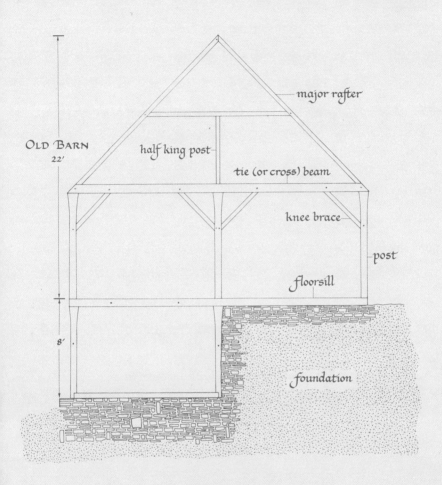

OLD BARN
22'

major rafter

half king post

tie (or cross) beam

knee brace

post

floorsill

8'

foundation

SOUTH ELEVATION

A
PLACE
in the
COUNTRY

A
PLACE
in the
COUNTRY

A Narrative on the Imperfect
Art of Homesteading
and the Value of Ignorance

PETER H. MATSON

Random House · New York

Grateful acknowledgment is made to the following for permission to reprint previously
published material:

From "The Return" by Ezra Pound, Copyright 1926, 1954 by Ezra Pound. Reprinted
by permission of New Directions Publishing Corporation.

From "In My Craft or Sullen Art" by Dylan Thomas, Copyright 1946 by New Directions
Publishing Corporation, renewed 1974 by Mrs. Caitlin Thomas. Reprinted by
permission of New Directions Publishing Corporation.

From "The Code" by Robert Frost, from The Poetry of Robert Frost, edited by
Edward Connery Lathem. Copyright 1930, 1939, © 1969 by Holt, Rinehart and
Winston. Copyright renewed 1958 by Robert Frost and renewed 1967 by Lesley Frost
Ballantine. Reprinted by permission of Holt, Rinehart and Winston Publishers.

Library of Congress Cataloging in Publication Data

Matson, Peter H
A place in the country.

1.   Matson, Peter H.   2.   United States—Biography.
I. Title.
CT275.M46446A35   974.4'1'040924 [B]   76-53470
ISBN 0-394-49591-8

Manufactured in the United States of America
9 8 7 6 5 4 3 2
First Edition

. . . What is most of our boasted so-called knowledge but a conceit that we know something, which robs us of the advantages of our actual ignorance.

For a man's ignorance sometimes is not only useful, but beautiful . . .

—HENRY DAVID THOREAU

Foreword

A few years ago I thought to find a place to live removed from the influences of the city, a simple place to be with my children on weekends, where vegetables would grow and water would come out of a well. Like many before me I soon discovered that what I wanted was a house like none I had ever seen, and that to realize it I would have to build it myself, with my own hands. For technical assistance a copy of Ramsey and Sleeper's *Architectural Graphic Standards* was kept close-by, but this immensely informative source book did not save me from making some sad and wonderful mistakes. I console myself—as would any contented fool— that such are the mirror of my ambition, myself irredeemably revealed, and that by writing them down there is a net gain in the final accounting.

The building process was far more intricate and educational than might be expected. I found a new pleasure in discovering the way ordinary things work—post and lintel, the thumb latch on the bathroom door, the Bank —and in turn the boundaries of the known world have expanded. That, also, is what this book is about.

The house is not "finished" at this writing, perhaps it never will be. My hope for it is that it will reflect the manner of its making in some way, that the roof will be more than a barrier to the stars, that the walls will grow old and out of plumb with a certain grace. Whether or not that has been accomplished, there are questions of quality, Progress, the culture's awesome talent for demeaning imitation, which followed immediately on my introduction to that wonderfully expanding landscape.

But make no mistake: this is a completely modern experience. I wouldn't have asked these questions just a few years ago, when technology beckoned us to a perfect, plastic-domed future. Now we have again been made terribly aware that value must be sought out, and if my response is to build "by hand," it is because that choice seems the most modern and obvious, made available by what the late technological era has bequeathed us. I wrap my eighteenth-century construction in four-mill polyethelene to keep out the damp; the heavy white oak and chestnut beams that hold the place together are treated with the latest insecticides, perhaps dangerously toxic to fibers grown in the age of Cotton Mather. Electric current pours into the house from many miles away, providing music, water and the cornerstone of the enterprise—a power saw. (Of course this house is built less by hand than any house built before the age of rural electrification.)

It is an awesome business, this shelter-building; enormous fun and an enormous headache. Remember to laugh at it now and then, and remember that the really good builders, the ones who give us our models, had the sense to be amateurs.

Contents

A
PLACE
in the
COUNTRY

I

Looking for Sanctuary

A day spent planting. Cold and dark in the morning, threatening still more rain. By eleven A.M. night seems to be falling, and I wonder if I shouldn't be building an ark up there rather than a house: it's been raining for a week. On top of a garden fence post there's an old tin light fixture, from the burned-down barn, I suppose: it makes a satisfactory ring when hit with the edge of the trowel. I bang on it, making sun-noises, making a symphony, sending hopeful rays of sound over the field to be picked apart by the wind and then thrust uselessly into the evergreens lining the far side of the field.

Still, by three o'clock patches of bluest sky come pell-mell over the hill, rain clouds rushing away to the coast pushed by a new north wind. On the other side of this small valley, different shades of green pursue each other and the popple at the bottom of the forsaken pasture seem to quicken their steps, knowing I watch with the eye of the enemy. (They have to go.) Above us, where the pasture starts, the pine tops are spitting in the gusts like surf, and the house seems about to launch itself downwind, to sail the Berkshires belly up, sloughing through the valleys, over the ridges.

According to the timetable of most of my predecessors on this farm, I am past middle age. I feel a child: how often since childhood have I spent the day doing that thing that excludes all others, that commands perfect attention? Too few, none perhaps like those lived since this homesteading started, this search for roots. Or is it just the exhilaration of the moment, night coming on and the garden started once again? In the wealth of this moment I wonder how many Americans are embarrassed by what they must do for "a living"; and I wonder what we can do for *life,* thus frozen by our hungers?

Building a house was my oldest fantasy, more familiar than sex: houses of blocks, of blankets, houses built with walls of air and roofs of it-never-rains. But since I was eighteen, I have always been a tenant some place. Living in other people's houses I have never been home, nor had any idea that I was missing something. To paraphrase Thoreau, I thought a house a prison in which I found myself oppressed and confined, not sheltered and protected . . .

Now I find a place of earth and air, trees, bugs, brambles, water, mud, lots of granite, a piece of planet that the White Man's Law says is mine. The joy realized is akin to the adolescent discovery of sexuality and no less complicated and all-pervasive. Or rather it is all very much the same thing: the discovery that we are—still—creatures of nature needing earth, air, privacy to sustain us, our drives and our perversions. The wreck of our Inner Cities is the negative testimonial.

Which for some reason brings me to money, a subject I would like to get out of the way. I carry minimal insurance, have never invested in anything (except a couple of signed first editions of novels I admired), have never put money away in savings accounts. These precautions seem loony to me; perhaps the search for such financial security is too close to a denial of life, through the attempt to accommodate death. But at the same time my life has been careful. For near half my years I have worked in New York City. I make enough money to support myself and five dependents who live elsewhere. I have not always been inspired by my work but sufficiently diligent, I believe, occasionally daring. Of course, when it came time to put money down, I might have wished that I had been born with a greater appreciation of compound interest. By some small miracle, however, I had accumulated credits sufficient to have some $12,000 available at the crucial moment. And that turned out to be enough, since I gladly go without whatever available luxury to pay the incessant bills from hardware store and lumberyard, not forgetting the mortgage. In short, this is not a rich man's operation; but money is not the major problem, either. The two essentials in short supply are time and patience, and if I could just find the one, I could do without the other.

And there is no lack of attention. It is almost as if I were in love with the place. A superb folly, I know. This ex-farm cares not what I do, provided sound husbandry rules. A rich man with a whim to see his once-active landscape reflower could make it happen without caring for the thing that caused his pleasure. Yes, the mind says, that is so; but underneath, in the same spectrum that signals satisfaction with the way the wet earth felt this afternoon, there is the sense that the earth is alive, not an inert thing no matter how often we treat it as such, thinking it gives no heed to our desecrations. The land is alive, this coming-to-earth says to me, and responds to care; it is a whole that mourns its diminution as it rejoices in fruitfulness; and it can shuck us off, maybe has before, when our presence gets annoying. (Or maybe it will just come apart and start all over again from the top; wouldn't take all that long, earthtime.)

The house is built on a granite ledge (some difficulties there!); the living rock pokes up at random in the field and is the geological basis of these hills. When you hit it with a pick or a shovel you know you're onto something solid, a floor without a cellar: it has the solid ring of eternity. But it is also the stuff that, broken down, is built up to the point that it's a-growin' my veg, just now; and dead grass decaying on the compost pile is as valuable as the live variety. Looking out across this field it is important to understand that it does have a life of its own somewhere, that this irascible house, incapable of being finished, is also "alive," growing out of the granite no less organically (if I could have it so) than the future veg, the maple trees, the fern at the field's edge. If that is not so, then to me it is just a mass of indistinguishable color down there, scenery out of time, a flickering screen.

That incantation was so successful that it has now rained for the last twenty-four hours, steady: two inches, the radio says. Fog sits in the valley, everything is wet, the new grass as green as plastic. After that brief show of sun, the wind flipped around, catching up the rain clouds, pushing up the valley at the exposed end of the house. When that happens the rain comes inside, running along the roof boards from the gable ends: they should be caulked and capped. (A fascia is what's missing; last fall I was glad enough to get the windows in, never mind the trimmings. It wouldn't take more than a morning to get it right, but obviously it can't be done in the rain, and it's the sort of thing that tends to be forgotten on good, clear working days.) As they fall, the drops of water catch the glare of the upper windows, starting from what would be an attic if there were floors. They look precious. Despite the ruinous effect of water, if such a leak could be tamed and led sedately out of the house, I think I'd leave it be. As it is, the efficacy of the roof is the first thing people ask about; and is it necessary for me to be able to say the right sort of thing with a straight face: "Tight as a drum," for instance.

It's been a while since this barn has been tight as a

drum. When I first saw it some miles north, standing alone in a field, it looked four square, of perfect dimensions. But in fact it had not been in use for years and the back side was going. Rot infected one section of it caused by a peculiar sort of dormer, perhaps for taking in hay, which leaked, perhaps no worse than here. But it had leaked for a long time, and the damage to an otherwise intact, usable, pre-Revolutionary antique was horrible to behold. All the more so when you think that excluding fire and rain there's no reason why these beams can't hold up for another two centuries, or long enough to be forever.

But everything about this place, good or bad, is so satisfactory that I can't understand how it could have gone so long without me, and why it took me so long to find it out. We get caught up in our ways of living, I guess. For years I went blindly toward the ocean whenever I could leave the city, until all those other people made it more trouble than it was worth. Now I have just come from a walk into the beech trees in back of the house, digging through the layers of decay at their feet, wondering if I could get some of that richness into the garden as mulch. As I look up, I see the wind bend about the topmost branches, up there halfway to a slice of moon; sunlight like strings of crystal. The sense of a complete world, the colors are the colors of everything, the smell of the dank soil is autumn and spring together. I suppose this wonderment could be city-bred, I mean naïve; I hope it is not transitory. In any case it is *having it* that has made it necessary to look so closely, to examine each flower, each change of light and mood.

And where is this? Berkshire County, Commonwealth of Massachusetts. Nine hundred forty-one square miles: Vermont on the north, Connecticut south, New York to the west; Springfield and Boston lie over "ye terrible trail through the Green Wood." The county has 159 souls per square mile (57 was the U.S. average in 1970, in case you haven't looked it up recently), but, despite its relative density, lots of space. The eastern portion of Berks lies in the Connecticut Valley watershed; however the Westfield River (the eastern county border) drains these hills, on account of a ridge running north and south which also about divides the county in half (I'm looking at its eastern flank), and all that over beyond the ridge to the west is in the Ousetonnuck Valley (a Mohawk name signifying "the place beyond the mountains"— "Housatonic" to you honkies). It is that western part that people think of when they think of this corner of the world at all: Tanglewood, rolling hills, fertile—once bountiful—farmland, Nathaniel Hawthorne, Melville, Stockbridge, Fanny Kemble. This town wasn't settled until the mid-1700's; the first town meeting was held to "chuse all such Town Officers as the Law directs and Requires" in 1765. (By contrast, the first townships of the Hudson Valley, now only an hour's drive away, were into their *second* century by that time.)

This was remote land, cut off from the traffic in the Connecticut and Hudson valleys by the "Green Woods" above-mentioned, through which the earliest travelers took an Indian trail; if they made twenty-five miles in a day's ride they did well. One Benj. Wadsworth (later president of Harvard) went out to treat with the assembled chiefs of the "Five Nations" in Albany in 1694. He wrote that the trail was "very woody, rocky, mountainous, swampy; extreme bad riding it was; I never yet saw so bad travelling. . . ."

Why would anyone bother, with so much other land available? Perhaps some of the immigrants to this western outpost were simply misled. They had heard about the Hudson Valley from soldiers returning east from the French-Indian wars. Were the reports somewhat exaggerated: streets paved with gold, with a little Holy Grail mixed in, perhaps lotus petals floating in a fountain of youth? We know the persistence of such myths—paradise somewhere for me, oh Lord (here?), some place where hungers and death don't have the price of admission. By the time the good yeoman had cleared the forest floor (burning it over mostly) and collected the rock, the myth had done its work. If the land was not what he had thought it would be, his complaints are lost to history and the myths soon forgotten, one hopes; at least until his son, or his grandson if he was lucky, hearing tales of the fertile valleys and inexhaustible topsoil to be found "out west" saddled up and rode into the sunset.

But the land was free, or almost free, to anyone willing to settle it. It's not hard to imagine that the land-hungry settler was not looking at it with a particularly critical eye, and in any case it was virgin land, untried; perhaps, under the mantle of the hardwood forests, it looked very much like the more fertile townships in the valleys to the south and west.

And there were all sorts of pressures building up on the coast: new immigrations, land speculation, the imagined need to wrest the still-wild territories from the heathen, the perhaps more understandable notion of setting up a buffer zone against the French and hostile Indians in Canada. The land was eventually claimed, though in some cases establishing a town with sawmill, meeting house, boundaries was the work of several decades (one imagines that those first forays into the wilderness might have been somewhat tentative; this township records that the business of finding a good site for the first mill —before the town was properly settled—was contracted out to three different people over a period of five years). But once they were started, most of these hill towns had what it took to fulfill the eighteenth-century requirements for a prosperous, self-contained community of hard-working, and fervently God-fearing (soon revolutionary) citizens.

Later there was a kind of Golden Age of Agriculture around here, lasting up to the Civil War, but not beyond. For example, Sandisfield, incorporated in 1762: in 1776 it had 1,044 inhabitants; in 1800, 1,857. In 1860, despite western emigration, the population held at 1,585. But changing times caught up with it then, and deserted farms pocked the landscape; by 1890 there were 807 people living there, and by the most recent count, only 547. At one time the township had fifteen cider distilleries, six tanneries, mills of all sorts (grist, saw, silk, wool); two stages linked it to Hartford and the Hudson River ports, which were its market places. (As I write there is no public transport regularly coming and going to Sandisfield.)

That sort of farming/industrial prosperity was never equaled by this township; nature did not intend it. But throughout the upland, in villages rich and poor and especially at the time of its adolescent flowering, there grew a pride of place, a separatism, that historians have defined as "provincialism." To me, it seems a not-unattractive quality.

Further definitions: the *Encyclopaedia Britannica* tells me that this is "an uplifted peneplain of subaerial denudation," although there is some evidence that suggests the basic platform was underwater at one time. In plainer language I understand this to mean that these are old hills, formed when a piece of the earth's crust was pushed up in some ancient geological holocaust. The underlying rock is mostly crystalline schists and gneisses, deformed and twisted in the creation and then worn down by time, wind and water. Bare stumps of their former selves, disorderly and "internally misshapen" (again the *E.B.*), they are now far advanced in their second cycle of weathering. The retreat of the last glacier gave this region its final form, of course, and in so doing helped create the county's political and social orientation.

The great *Encyclopaedia* of 1906 goes on, calling Berkshire County "one of the most picturesque regions in America, consisting of range after range of hills, with broad and fertile valleys intermingled, and with innumerable streams and lakes to add charm to the prospect."

The most recent edition is somewhat more restrained. This is "a degraded mountain system," it says, "whose stoney soil is unsuitable for advanced agriculture." Rhapsody has no place in current encyclopedic fashion.

But of course they are right, those realists at the modern *E.B.* In the closing years of the nineteenth century Massachusetts citizens raised better than 90 per cent of the food they ate; today they raise less than 10 per cent. There are only 380 farms in Berkshire County, or were at the last federal count in 1969; they average 212 acres, and 158 of those farms had sales for that year of *less than $2,500.*

The state has about doubled in population since 1900, and in the same time farm acreage has dwindled from 2.1 million acres in 1945, to 710,000 in 1970. I didn't bother to look up food prices; we all know what's happened. But the small farmer was never organized, was never able to protect his market place, had no lobbyists in Washington, was never even a recognizable voting bloc. The frontiersman's dream of a stable, self-sufficient community, peace and plenty and independence (also justice, when it wasn't altogether inconvenient) came and went too quickly; hardly anybody noticed. Yet it was a worthy dream, even counting the misuse of the land and its native inhabitants, the greed that sapped the spirit, the unceasing hard work in pursuit of God's undiscoverable grace.

As I wrote that last, contradictory sentence a blue bird with white and black markings on its back, six or seven inches long, was running down lunch on a silver birch in the woods at my right. I saw the same bird in the forest a couple of days ago, down by the stream, climbing around the hemlock, up one, down the next, hard at work. Lots of birds this morning; a red-throated warbler and two mourning doves have decided that the space out front (not quite what you'd call lawn) offers special delicacies. Dragged from my desk by curiosity, I finally traced the source of an outrageously high-pitched, clearest birdsong. It was coming from the branches of one of the ruined apple trees in the field, so small that I saw the bird for what it was only when it threw back its head to sing. Given equal efficiency, the human vocal chords would be a weapon of horrible potentiality.

Two deer strolled slowly across the bottom of the field the other morning, perhaps mother and young—they were gone so fast I couldn't be sure. The next, a lone doe came up to the garden as I was working, the sun just poking through the trees. I felt it first, a large, moving warmth; looking up I saw a head above the bushes, lots of ears, then heard the strangely hard tattoo as she fled into the woods, leaving behind an erratic trail of fear. In truth, she only thought to run a split second before I could get my own legs working, which may be the reason we hunt deer, and not the other way round.

I don't know. Like most Americans, I was never properly instructed in the construction of the real world: when I was getting my education, "nature" was not a subject considered necessary or proper to a young man's preparation for life, and "ecology" had not yet been discovered. I spent my early childhood in the country

(the first night ever spent in a city is a deep memory—
mysterious and wonderful music of the traffic in the
street below), and nature interested me. But it was not
available to study. Perhaps it was too much just there.
When I started looking for sanctuary I began to see how
much I had missed, how much I didn't know. Thus the
towns got smaller and smaller, the city farther away, the
roads less and less well traveled.

The road to this hilltop, hardscrabble farm is still
gravel. The first time I saw it was late September two
years ago. As we wound through some second-growth
woodland the road climbed, almost imperceptibly at
first, then more rapidly as fields appeared on either side
(overgrown it's true, but recognizable as recently working land). A proud border of old maples marched up the
last rise, their leaves translucently yellow in the afternoon sun, along their base a stone wall almost disappearing again into the earth. The agent got us out into a field
high with the uncut summer's growth. At the crest of the
hill was a thicket of blackberry and sumac. The stone
foundation of the small farmhouse was collapsing into its
pit; here and there were the signs of a destroying, cleans-
ing fire.

"Was a pig farm once," said the agent; then, perhaps
thinking he had started off on the wrong foot, pointed
across the field. "There's a stream down there some-
wheres . . ."

Across the small intervale we looked two or three
miles, I reckoned, to a range of hills speckled and shining
in the autumn quiet. Promising; but closer at hand the

field seemed too common for the fancy price I had been quoted.

"Could be divided, of course." Real estate agents always know when the prospect is thinking money, and they often hold out such a softening proposition. Subdivision gets to be another way of life, I guess, but it was the maples that had my attention, and the sun playing on their rich colors, and the sinking wall. No sense of history peopled the landscape for me then; still, a common, felt heritage insisted that someone had planted those trees, and someone had dragged those stones out of the field, with sled and oxen perhaps; the track barely perceivable through shoulder-high goldenrod was the result of God knows how many hours of man and animal sweat. Yes, there was that which seemed right about the place, but at the same time something also repelled. Was it too much of that sense of farmwork come to naught, the land still harboring the spirits of tired homesteaders making untidy departures for flatter, darker fields? Or just too much ordinary garbage about? The driveway past the old foundation, eroded by recent rains, revealed some broken and crushed toys, plastic still hopelessly bright; the torso and head of a small rubber doll, dirty and rather pig-like. I felt no impulse to walk across that field into the woods, sniff around its corners; impressions then only dimly, even subliminally received confused the circuits perhaps.

I remarked, safely, that there seemed to be a nice view, anxious to get back, to get to the next place, yet feeling a bit apologetic for taking this conscientious man so far out of his way. But my car was sitting in front of his roadside office, back in the wrong direction. Agents do that. They all insist on driving you in their car, imprisoning you, conducting a tour that has very little to do with your carefully worded descriptions of a dream. "An old, broken-down farmhouse at the end of a lot of dirt road," I would say, wanting him to take me to that place he had decided would never sell, forgotten, forlorn; the house innocent of wiring, the walls puffy with age, a privy privately falling in on itself. The answer comes back: "I know just what you mean" and "Let's take my car." Many miles later there is a neat stucco cottage just at the edge of a two-lane highway with privet hedges guarding the door and a two-car garage around back, underneath. The picture window—this really happened, by the way— faces the road, not the worst view in the world given the pasture beyond, except that the cement works at the bottom of the hill send forth a couple of dozen fourteen-wheeled trucks several times a day, and of course they need every one of their thirty-six gears for the pull past the privet hedges. At last I found it was better to do the thing negatively: "No stucco, no picture windows, above all no cement works." Also I gave over my jaunty week-end livery for a faded workshirt and jeans. No less studied, but image is everything in the game of buy and sell, and like a good gambler at dining-car poker it is important to look just a little off-hand, yet decisive. The agent is not taken in, but he appreciates that you know the finer points and will treat you accordingly. On the other hand, if I did this over again (God doesn't dislike me that much) I would work the whole thing backwards. It is comforting to put the process in the hands of a professional; but wasteful of time and energy. I suppose that too many people don't really know what they want, or get talked into something, or settle for less than what their dream has vouchsafed to them; whatever the reason, real estate agents *don't believe you.* The only way to get down to serious business is to find the village, town or valley that interests you, find out what might be for sale and who can show it to you. There's always something someone wants to sell.

At that time I was well into my second year of trying to talk to real estate agents and beginning to think the dream would not materialize in any of the permutations it had taken. The foraging area had thus been expanded; the *New York Times* ads decoded with ever-increasing accuracy, visits programed with a map and mileage charts. Already that day we had seen several other impossible places; one a huge rambling pile of shingles and fieldstone with wonderfully overgrown, once-formal gardens, a poolroom and, in a corner of the basement, a bowling alley. In the orchard the trees were bare, the apples wormy but pressable: they lay on the ground to rot. It was the irrational 1920's remnant of a bootlegger's mountain retreat; one thinks that anyway the architect must have had fun. As for the bowling alley: "Wait till you see this," said the agent in the tones of a snake-oil salesman hawking Health Everlasting for only 99 cents (and satisfaction guaranteed in this life or the next). It was regulation size, properly fitted out with chairs and ashtrays. A ball sat in the return alley and two pins stood way down yonder. I don't know from bowling, but it was obvious that to hit them both with one ball would take pinpoint accuracy. Who could have resisted? The ball felt heavy, skidded, avoided the alley, hooked at the right millisecond, and I had 'em both. I thought it a very good omen. But now, older and wiser, I harbor a suspicion that the alley had a groove in it, that the salesman was even more resourceful than I first supposed. Surely, as the pins dropped, I was a buyer.

Running up the stairs after the agent (he hadn't stopped to watch), I yelled: "How much is this place anyhow?" And having his answer thought: maybe I should rob a bank.

The press for "second houses" was dropping off then, and I think this guy had time on his hands. He as much as told me that he had put the ad in the Sunday *Times* out of boredom; his usual line of work was dealing in ruined chateaux, viz., the above. In fact I was as desperate as the seller and his agent, or the ad would never have been clipped. In my experience "wooded acs. w/stream" could have described a pine grove in a marsh where only a Bornean tribesman could find an accommodating building site. But I had driven through the town and knew it had a nice old church (which I now know to be a library), and a later but still-imposing Grange. And even after that first visit it was the road to the parcel ("the parcel" is to real estate language what "the property" is to motion pictures) that I remembered, rather than the land itself. The land didn't measure up to the places of my imagination, where houses were nestled perfectly among giant sequoia at the edge of a national forest—perhaps in the Alps—or perched on the bank of a Norwegian fjord, the glassy water reflecting only the surrounding peaks and a fishing boat moored a line's throw from the shore.

I guessed it would be required that I first dispel the dream of America's past before my own could come tumbling into view. (We have no collective dreams of the future. Nothing to decipher our wealth, our machines, our ability to produce; nothing to tell us what our work is for or give us words to define the American Way in moral terms.) Instead of the fantasies that are the baggage of my growing, I saw that afternoon a quality that had been dug into the earth, spread with the manure from those swine: the ambitions of that first, possibly misguided pilgrim looking for redemption. Stumbling onto it, I was stuck with it. And so my own future started to change—in midflight, one might say.

I had to begin to think clearly about housing, shelter, money. I had some notion of land prices and mortgage costs, but everyone who built, I knew, always ended up the servant of a dozen creditors, owning a house that wasn't really theirs. Fifteen years before, I had done some building, carpentry, plumbing: summer jobs. Some confidence was retained from that experience and others —doing the obvious to impossible city apartments, making space, erasing the previous tenant's life. I would have to call on all these resources. I wouldn't be able to back into the shelter business, courtesy of that forlorn, tough old house of oak frame hidden under years of genteel misuse.

I tried once more though. It was in New York State, and I think that the agent who showed it was violating the secret code, because it had possibilities. A squat but not ungraceful farmhouse of uncertain vintage, fields overgrown, fruit trees out back still laden with wizened fruit and worms, the privy strangled with poison ivy or grape —I couldn't get close enough to tell. It had a damp Southern charm on a hot fall day; but the past owners had grown old there, their children had gone off to become accountants or barge people, the farm failing with the parents' failing strength. The winter before, part of the kitchen had burned, and with no place else to go (one imagines) the old couple departed the material plane; but not the premises, I felt. That they didn't really want to sell yet seemed a logical and healthy supposition.

A couple of weeks later, in need of a place to picnic and not a little curious for a second impression, we—myself and wife and infant son—headed back to the town with the church on the corner. I noticed that the gravel road ("gd. town maint. rd.," as the ads say) started with a small bridge over a stream. There seemed to be quite a lot of water in it, tumbling appropriately over its rocky bed and on the other side running down into a kind of chasm. The road went on for longer than I had remembered, the maples were a deeper, golden yellow. When we reached the top of the hill the field had somehow shrunk, like a room of one's childhood.

We left the car by the side of the road, and set out to

discover the less obvious values of the place, perhaps even find its farthest border. (The agent hadn't quite known where it was: not his line of work.) It was cold. The sun came and went behind high cumulus. We ate quickly, taking comfort from the occasional bursts of warmth, our son determined to crawl off the blanket, to get at the grass, the ants; everything needed testing in his rapacious mouth. He definitely liked what he saw/touched. We felt remote; the view grew more spectacular as it became more familiar. At the brow of the hill, camouflaged by those sumac and blackberry canes, guarded by a picket line of young poplar, was a bit of stone wall. Surely this was the foundation of the barn once, and just as surely here was the place to put a house! But no, farther back, where the trees had stood for a while (maples, perhaps a sugarbush), there were the remains of some other outbuilding: a house here could peek out of the trees at the valley and hills beyond.

Child on hip, I walked down into the idle pasture, into the afternoon sun and shadow. At the far edge we moved through a thicket of new deciduous trees, offspring of the grand maple, beech and birch that once comprised the fence line. They spread a good fifty to sixty feet onto land that had been grazed just twelve years before. Behind them was another crumbling stone wall and the entrance to the evergreens. I had to go through the first bit backwards to keep the branches from the baby's face, and then found that in the forest itself the trees were big enough to walk under without difficulty. It was wet underfoot, and the darting sun made patches of green here

LOOKING FOR SANCTUARY

and there on the rolling forest floor; the sound of the wind in the treetops was far away. Fern and mushroom and brambles in the openings, and farther away than we had thought, the stream cut a meandering swath, banks quite high, water puzzlingly sparse. Was this the edge of the property? If so there was a lot more to forty-eight acres than I thought.

This section of forest had been cut over, of course, but not for some time, from the look of the mossy, decaying stumps. Obviously it had never been cleared: it was primeval. We sat by the stream getting the feel of it, listening, waiting for magic; sparks that were sunlight fell into the water; soon it was saying, "Buy me, buy me, buy me . . ." (Or was it: "By me! By me!" Why are my voices so ambiguous?)

Having caught the siren song, whatever its intention, I began an immediate, characteristic retreat. "Wait a minute. Let's look at this thing calmly." But walking back through the firs too quickly we were disoriented (I think: I always know where I'm going), lost for a moment, finally getting to the field scratched and winded (the baby asleep in my arms) far below our original path. Something had happened, time deflected. I needed a horse to gallop the boundaries. I wanted to set up camp, my head full of plans for shelter to keep off the rain, trap heat in the winter, a place to cook and sleep and love.

Practical thoughts were chased away again by another look at the hills from our picnic ground. They were the amazing colors everyone expects in a New England autumn. As the clouds' shadows raced over them, they

seemed to draw forward, then receded, pulsating, a mul-
ticolored minuet set to earth rhythm. (The prospect con-
tains its own inevitable rebuke: we see, register timeless-
ness, let go of self for a blind moment. Then, locking our
insignificance in the vault of the mind, turn away sad and
impressed.)

So this ex-hog farmer now living somewhere in the
Midwest wants $26,000 for his lousy forty-plus acres. In
actual money he will accept $10,000, with the remainder
over ten years at a mortgage rate of (only) 7 1/2 per cent.
Good terms if the land were worth it. The ten G's are
about what I can see in the crystal ball without hurting
the eyes.

I said $20,000 (why not) and he said no. We were
negotiating! I felt a little light in the head and thought
a lot about getting drunk. It took a while to answer. I
asked, mind if I take another look at the goods, thinking
some fresh value might be perceived—oil perhaps. This
time the agent had done some homework; I went up one
weekday to "walk the boundaries" with him. Disappoint-
ments: The western boundary was the field's edge, not
the stream deep in the woods. (He laughed.) The stream
itself contributed less than half the volume of that more
vigorous specimen down the valley. Three acres from
the top had been sold off a couple of years previous, and
the telephone company had a right of way for an underground cable through one corner. The lot lopped off was
the most disturbing: I didn't take to the idea of settling
in tandem with a stranger. The right of way was some-

what comforting, as if it gave the land a special sort of validity.

But then we got down into the woods again, above the spot I'd already explored. The land has an odd arm that sticks out to the west, over the stream and up the other side of its valley. As we pushed through the evergreens (smaller here, this part was once pasture), we were suddenly confronted by a marsh of several acres manufactured by a most industrious clan of beaver. The dams had been broken through by the State Forestry people, who don't much appreciate the kind of landscaping the beavers specialize in, and the remains of the beavers' pond was no more than thirty yards across, but the openness they had created was as welcome as a gasoline shortage in the city. The stream spilled through the old dam with surprising force, then cut a respectable channel through what could almost pass for a meadow. I caught a glimpse of a brown trout almost four inches long. "Trout!" said the agent, knowing he had hit on another secret word. And a red-winged blackbird perched on a tuft of grass just where he should have been. (Was he stuffed, I wonder?) Remote, peaceful, better than oil. The dam was fully fifty paces long and six feet high from the downstream side; other, smaller dams had been established along the course, succeeding generations setting out. Then more hardwoods on another old piece of pasture, bordered by more stone walls. (Wouldn't these wall-builders be surprised at what they have done for land prices?)

Later I said $22,500, thinking I might make a pond

where the beavers had so successfully managed theirs. But I wanted the seller to negotiate a right of first refusal if that other guy ever wanted to sell, and I wanted the whole surveyed. I waited impatiently, not knowing if I was hoping for a yes or a no. The answer came back from the Midwest, via the agent, in what I imagined were stentorian tones: "Twenty-four thousand and no crap about surveyors or protective covenants." (Was that what I was asking for?)

Back in the city it was getting cold, and the whole idea equally remote. So this time I said no. It felt a sound and sensible decision made up of equal parts business sense (Seller was obviously in great need and no one else would come along before spring), Puritan self-denial, and confusion. Also my wife was very much against it, for reasons that will come out later, perhaps.

What a relief! To hell with it! Two days later I wasn't so sure. Everything I read, everyone I talked to, kept reminding me that three years before you could have had the same for half the price, and that three years from now it would double again. It was the year of buy. And didn't I trust my senses and the gods in the trees? I called back and suggested, rather weakly, that in order to make the deal right away I would go to $23,000. Hanging up, I knew I'd been had. Already seller and his agent were on the long distance having a good laugh and thinking up still craftier swindles. But no answer came back.

Acting as I thought a prospective landowner should, I went to take yet another look. By this time there was snow on the ground. The deserted beaver ponds were frozen, even more isolated from machine and man. Walking along the brook, listening to the water under the ice, I imagined a house on the hill up there, a fire going, a hot beaker of something spicy and perhaps intoxicating steaming on the hearth. The afternoon sunlight would be slanting in big windows, making odd patterns on walls framed by old beams. Perhaps thatch on the roof—no, that was going too far. But I felt sure that whatever was up there had to have grown old *in situ:* I would have to build a place that was already a bit round-shouldered, stooped with age, one of those barns that seem to be siblings to the granite walls that so often surround them. And of course there was the old barn foundation . . . It had started to snow very quietly in the woods, the flakes drifting down, taking their time choosing a place to land.

But nothing was heard from the great Midwest. For a while I was a pilgrim without destination.

In the meantime I ran into the Three Acres, who turned out to look just like a human being. He had a wife and small children and a site picked out on the other side of the road; he had lived on the old farmstead as a child. I thought we might eventually be friends.

Then, thinking to allay lingering misapprehensions, I paid a visit to a local surveyor. Well, of course I had to understand that nothing could be done now until spring (oh God, of course!), and then the job would have to wait in line, and anyway her husband (he wasn't there but she seemed to have things well in hand) was getting on and didn't do as much as he used to. Their house was solid and staid in the way of the 1920's: there were plastic covers on the living-room furniture. The surveyor's wife was in real estate, it appeared: she owned some land up that very road, quite a lot of it, in fact, everything from Tennessee Avenue to Marvin Gardens. She seemed just a little annoyed that a property had slipped through her hands.

She asked me how much. Does one say? I thought: truth is always the best policy, naïveté will see me through. Naming the seller's figure caused no discernible reaction. She talked for a bit of what prices used to be; she asked had I heard about the new highway coming up the valley. Well, seemed like it would wipe out that stream and all. Anyhow the road was going to be paved on account of the development; the town couldn't keep it plowed as it was. Water was hard to come by on the hill, she had heard. She had some maps. Had I looked at the lakesites available ($3,000 the half acre)? I listened somewhat open-mouthed. Was this woman doing me a favor, warning me off in good-neighborly fashion, trying to spare my simplicity? Or was I being slicked (my years of commerce with her colleagues had taught me something). Perhaps she wanted me to believe she believed I had been taken to the cleaners so she could snarfle up my land when I turned my back? But then again she might be a step ahead of me, feigning interest in this negative fashion, thus cementing the sale and making her own worthless acres saleable to other city dolts, perhaps my hapless friends and innocent relatives? I still don't know, but hope that she had meant to drive me away with a bold frontal attack, no strategy, no subtlety, simple superiority of arms.

I left feeling somehow fortified, even victorious. Her aim had been off. And was that the Surveyor himself coming out of the woodshed, somewhat bent, painfully loading a sled with kindling?

Surveying seemed to make no sense after that. I knew where the land was and what it was. Counting it was an arbitrary procedure, and it would cost lots. I tried to figure out the square footage from the agent's map and laid that on a kind of graph somebody worked out.

I went back to the city and thought about it some more. I sat on people's floors (a good place to contemplate ruin) and talked myself into it, or tried to. Then a letter came from the agent. He wrote: "Why not give your talent for masochism a rest? You know he'll get his price in the spring." He enclosed a sixty-day option to buy at $24,000. I signed it the same day and returned it with a check for $500, thinking, well, that's how it's done. Then I went home to break the bad news.

That agent is now selling land in Florida, I believe. It's said he is doing well.

So it *was* done. I called friends to find a lawyer who could do the small necessaries without being simply annoyed. The money was raised, the papers signed without a hitch. I went back before the end of February and walked around with the names of former owners in my head: Besquet, Morgan, Attwood, Gross. I didn't feel like a landowner. I felt scared. I felt a responsibility, not to Grimace, the mortgage-holder, but to the land and its past pilgrims. I wanted to show that I would do the right sort of thing by it, nothing drastic, that if someone would show me the ropes I would prove a fast, sympathetic learner.

I cut brambles with the blade of a shovel bought at a roadside "used furniture and antiques" place. I paced out the distance between trees. The snow melted, the field emerging again in its grey March coat. I made a mortgage payment; my wife thought I was nuts, that I had developed a taste for bankruptcy. I felt rich in choices, possessed of neolithic ambitions; if it was wrong I would know about that sometime in the future. I woke every morning looking for spring.

II

The Invisible Journey

Land. Landsman. Landed, or maybe landing. Back to the land. The lay of the land. The land of milk and honey. Bad lands, timberland, farmland. Earth that can be picked up, smelled, felt, contemplated, taken to the state agricultural service for chemical analysis, posted with No Trespassing signs, misused, worn by some like a psychic skin. The land survives us, tolerates us: we were the land before the land was ours (apologies to Robert Frost). Land, ho! A night on the land.

The first night, there was snow on the ground. Late March: when we came over the mountain into our valley, the cold rain that had been falling intermittently turned to snow. I have never made camp in the snow; in the back of the car were two small tents and all my dependents,

ranging in age from fourteen to one. (Back to the land!)
It was almost dark. We drove up the gravel road, the
headlights picking up the wet snow on the stone wall, the
wind blowing hunks of it off overhanging branches onto
the hood of the car.

I stopped along the side of the road, but there was no
great rush to get out of the warmth. I thought: how
reluctantly children are herded to adventure: mush
along now. The wind slashed at us as we climbed up to
the top of the hill. My laggard companions said: "I'm
cold," and "I'm freezing," and "Is this for *real?*" I had
thought that the ground under the snow and maple
leaves might be dry enough. (Both the tents had bottoms, but you're not advised to pitch them in a puddle,
I believe.) I found that the land was wrapped in wet
cotton wool—there wasn't anything dry above bed rock.
It was without doubt a very cold night. The baby, asleep
up to then in the back of the car, woke up, making plain
immediately that he didn't like the look of things at all.
I thought of Crazy Horse retreating from the Tongue
through drifts up to a horse's belly (it's said), the Conti-
nentals at Valley Forge leaving bloody footprints in the
snow. I wrapped myself in long furs and a beard . . . but
it's no use, you know. We are all junkies of technology:
as we plunged through the enveloping darkness looking
for some miraculously dry and protected campsite, the
image of a warm, windproof motel room pushed all others aside. When I realized that there would be no way
that we would be able to build a fire that night, a strategic
retreat was allowed. I turned the car around with diffi-

culty, calculating the cost of one more night in a motel as a cost increase, on the overall project, of something like .0004 per cent.

Backtracking to the twentieth century, to central heat and hot water, made shelter seem even more urgent. I had been listening to people say to take it slow, get a feel for the land, get to know it, don't rush into something so permanent. (And that is what I would tell somebody now.) But as we drove back down the road I built a dozen different shelters, thinking of ways to make it possible to be there, on the land, feeling defeated, unable to provide for my dependents' simplest needs. A wickiup, a cave, a lean-to in front of a bonfire, whatever it was to be, quickly; should it please the Fates.

The first shelter I ever built was made from branches ripped off the pitchpine behind a Cape Cod house. These were woven together in whatever manner the material would allow, and covered with dry needles. Elegant for an eight-year-old you might think, but the weaving was ad hoc and the red-brown thatch elegant but haphazard. It sounds better than it was, a pile of brush made into a place in which to be invisible. These huts had some good qualities: from a distance they merged completely with the woods, and when newly thatched they managed to keep out the wind and the first minutes of rain. Inside I remember a wonderful light.

But they didn't last. It was near unbearably sad to go back to one after a bit of weather: the pile of sticks with a few pine needles hanging from them was just enough to remind you of what once seemed possible there; the dreams of privacy, liberty. (I wanted some place of my own that would outlast a three day nor'easter.)

Thinking it through, a tent, teepee or leanto wasn't good enough. I needed "permanence," and some place to contain Fire. And once the human animal starts to think of fireplaces, cooking and warmth, any temporary shelter tends to get more and more permanent. Confronting this problem I had figured out a one-room cabin using $4' \times 8'$ sheets of (the cheapest) plywood and regular $2'' \times 4''$ framing, no windows, but a $4' \times 8'$ deck out front for a cost in material of about $750, including a factory-made sliding door. All the wood could be used over again, or the cabin kept as a kind of guest house or studio. Again, I advise such a plan, but it did not satisfy me; I could find no energy for it. I wanted, needed, insanely insisted on getting on with the real thing, ready or not. I reasoned that delaying was as good as not doing it at all; that the point is made by action, by taking the risk. The plunge into cold, unknown waters.

Choices had to be made, decisions from which there would be no appeal. Was it to be a dome, a yurt, a tower, a hole in the ground (into which you would pour a lot of concrete, making an interior court, etc.), a barn? Sorting out those entirely different possibilities is the conundrum we leave to our architects, perhaps their principal function, allowing us rank amateurs to think we are avoiding the rejection of unknowable attractions. In fact, aren't we mostly being led through a maze of someone else's prejudices? For me even buying a tent involves dozens of aesthetic and practical decisions, intense soul searching, astrological consultations and new investigations of my genealogy. So I build this house this way in order not to have to think about possible alternatives? Yes. As I couldn't get interested in doing something temporary, honing skills and computing relative costs; there was nothing left to do but do it.

While I was investigating all those unsuitable, made-over houses, what I came to remember were the barns, when they still existed; old drama standing in afternoon sunlight, swaybacked, waiting (wishing for?) the stock to return from the fields. And cheap as they stood, all that timber . . .

Recently I've noticed that every other issue of *House Beautiful* features some fashionable lady's newly remodeled carriage house, the hand-hewn beams so positively highlighted by a fashionable piece of Minimal Art. And I know a number of barns, boathouses, turkey coops that make do rather well for summer houses and studios. But a working or even a deserted barn is another sort of thing. Its plainness is its eloquence. It is to architecture what jeans are to fashion and for the same reasons: there is no way to "improve" a barn. Once they are messed about with they are less of a thing, alas. Surely the New England barn is one of the world's finest forms of vernacular architecture.

For instance, here was a large, endomorphic shape in back of a made-over farmhouse in the Hudson Valley, across a small stream. Where there had been a bridge, we forded on impromptu stepping stones. As we approached, the structure grew enormous, its lines hidden by the inevitable maze of poison ivy and sumac. Inside the sunlight filtered through splintered siding, rafters rocketed into ecclesiastical space; the dusty darkness was alive with the incense of ripe disuse, more harmonious here than in any church. Anchor beams thicker than they were deep, looking two feet and better in each dimension though my eye must have exaggerated, pulled it all together. Sixteen feet long they were: sixty-four cubic feet of what? Oak or white pine felled in the virgin forests just outside the barn door, squared with broadaxe and adze, hot work in that first summer's sun—homespun rolled up on the arms, cutting edges hot to touch when put to the stone. These Nieuwe Holländische farmers built their barns right off; sometimes, I read, seven harvests came in these huge doors before they felt it time to improve the log cabin that sheltered their families.

Where a rose window could have been, a loading door swung open, lighting up a rotting corner the ivy intended to pull down—nature's slow revolution. The upper purling sprung from its corner mortise like an acrobat caught stretching for a trapeze just out of reach; always out of reach now; in time it will fall into a net of brambles and rusted metal.

It is an abstraction, this barn; it has the majesty of deposed monarchs. A brilliant relic of a time when faith was its own reward, an unquestioned setting of roots for and against the eternal hereafter. If that corner could be fixed (that list to westward), this barn would last another two, three hundred years without so much as a heavy breath.

Look how this one joint is fastened together: cross-beam (anchorbeam, some say, or greatbeam) into post, tiebeam between posts, three supporting struts (knee braces) in this *one* connection (of hundreds), eight different joinings, sixteen different fastenings of tenon and mortise, all tightly pegged and wedged in tough oak or chestnut by hand!—and summer no longer for them than it is for us. (I reckon that working with hand tools only, after some practice, I might be able to manage to complete two such mortised joints in a *long* day's work.) The very best achievements of modern architecture seem pornographic in comparison.

Up there in the loft, the timbers have been polished by centuries of hay, a gold/yellow/rose. Climbing up on a loft we come on chairs, a table, a turn-of-the-century rocker with its upholstery in bits. Wallpaper peels from a corner that must have been fitted out as quarters for a hired man; in the evening the cows moved about in the managers below, taking the edge off loneliness perhaps.

It is a temple to the considered life, progeny, work done for its own sake,

> Not for ambition or bread
> Or the strut and trade of charms
> On the ivory stages
> > (D. Thomas)

and a wonderful denial of death, even as it sinks slowly into the rich manure around its sills.

That afternoon, sunlight dancing through the dust, I thought of returning in the night with a host of candles.

The space became baronial, a fieldstone fireplace sprung up in the nave, the dark corners filled with ghosts and dogs; men in leather jerkins and women in robes trimmed with fur moved about silently, listening to the wind in the battlements. How quickly fantasy rises from the old straw, replacing broken farm machinery and the scratching sounds of desertion. Instead of driving lamely to an overheated motel room, I wanted to enter such a hall amidst this crowd of family, be greeted by the spirits of some well-past life, rejoice that the enemy was beyond the stout walls, marching down other corridors, other valleys.

But a lot of thought was given to competing ideas nonetheless. Domes, dugouts, "modern designs," all were rejected on the ground that gabled roofs are more natural to the human being; that they more closely echo the space that homo erectus occupies, the "roof line" being the plane from the top of our pointy heads, touching the shoulder and continuing along the upper arm as we stand with hands on hips. I have tried living in a dome but never felt comfortably sheltered in one, and have heard the same from many others. (That they are difficult to build so that they don't leak is another sort of problem, not one—as you'll have gathered—that would deter me if it were a structure otherwise attractive.) And I have grown to like a roof pointing to the stars, not trying vainly to mimic the vault of heaven. I like the walls growing out of the ground straight, like a tree reaching for sunlight, and rafters making order of this small universe, the linear roof ridge indicating north and south.

Having gotten that far, it was short giant steps to the idea of moving a barn. I had heard of a man who moved barns for a living—his own house a Dutch barn he had moved to a spectacularly unbarn-like setting on top of a hill in a neighboring town—and had gone to see him on one of those weekend trips. He turned out to be a friendly, fiery, energetic man with lots of children running about. He boasted that he could tell the age of any barn within a decade by the numbering system on the timbers. (For those who don't know, the old way of putting a barn together was to lay it all out on the ground first, each join numbered, peg the section together on the flat, then raise it all in place, using block and tackle and long pikes.) He was immensely proud of his own place, his showplace. His father had been a sometime carpenter who, I gathered, had spent most of his life as a farmer, and thanks to the aggressive instincts of various psychopaths of our times had saved enough in the service of his government to leave his son a parcel of farm land. His son was an inventive man: he had sunk a huge old water tank into the mountainside in front of the house—filled with water it was bigger and cheaper than an ordinary swimming pool. On its first site the barn had rotted along the roof ridge, so he had expediently cut off the top quarter of the rafters, making a kind of bastard hip-roof. (It would not have looked right to the original builders.) Inside, the space was alarming and intriguing. The central fireplace had a hearth about five feet off the floor, the fire just at eye level. He explained the advantages: no stooping to feed the fire; impossible for small children to fall therein; no sitting in front, staring idly into the fireplace; mostly it was just "different."

Ranged about the mountainside in back of his place were several sheds containing the components of various barns pulled apart (de-pegged, I suppose you might say) and waiting to be something again. I described the huge Dutch farm in carefully modulated tones, lest he think me especially greenhorn. He was surprised there was such a structure standing unbeknownst to him and wondered if it might be for sale. He wanted to see it immediately. By the approximate measurements (45'×50' he guessed right away that it must be early eighteenth century, "a classic." He reckoned that if no one was taking care of it they might be glad to see it go, though he always paid his suppliers something on general principles. Still he wasn't prepared to say how much it might be worth or how much it might cost to take it down and put it back together again. Those darned farms are BIG, he said, and disappointed me by suggesting that I might want to use just two or three sections of it, perhaps.

Later I called the real estate woman and wondered if the Dutch barn could be bought without the cheaply modernized house. She said why not buy both and sell the house, keeping a right of way to the barn: it would be so nice with the stream going by and all. In any case it was perfectly all right to have someone take a look. A week or so later my new friend had had his look. I held my breath; what did he think? Well, it seemed that darned thing was exactly what I said it was, and more. He could even move it for $10,000–$12,000 roughly, replacing the few rotten members. But that didn't include the cost of buying the structure. Offer them a thousand, he said, and again: you know, it's one *great hunk* of a barn.

After another surreptitious inspection I tracked down the owners in New York. I talked lovingly about the great antique sitting in their backyard. They knew; they were getting a divorce; they wanted to sell the whole property. Trying not to make a moral case of it, I wondered if they realized that the roof was going: terrible how destructive rain can be. My voice trailed off hopefully. Talk to my wife's lawyer, the man said; the place had been a mistake. The lawyers were killing him; what could he do? Clearly his problems spelt the death of another irreplaceable monument; still, some monuments, like some dreams, die slowly in the material world. I had so much invested in this one, I thought it couldn't help but lead somewhere.

Somewhat heavy-hearted, I made another pilgrimage to the expert on the top of the hill. He was eating marshmallows out of a cellophane bag, children eyeing him hungrily. He suggested I look at some other sort of place. That was a mighty big barn I had my eye on. What did I figure to spend overall? Had I any i-dear what the price of lumber had got to? 'Course it was a prize, that one, absolute genuine real antique Dutch barn he guessed to be from the 1600's. There was both sales-talk and caution in his enthusiastic voice, and I picked up the discrepancy in his earlier dating with some misgiving. I knew what he was telling me, but I liked the dream even more if it was completely impractical; too often in my life

I had modeled ambition to another's advice. He understood this, was certainly not going to talk himself out of a job. So the barn raiser launched a long story about the time someone was rustling his calves during his years as a farmer, and how he laid ambush and took after them with an axe handle.

In the meantime another weekend was passing, the sun isolating the snow drifts by the side of the road. In a week or two there would be a green haze on the land, and I would still be wondering what I was going to do for shelter. Impatience gnawed at the base of my skull: something had to be started. I was determined to be roasting a turkey in my own oven on the appropriate Thursday in November, if not before.

In the silence that greeted the end of his story, my friend suggested that he show me a couple of alternatives. We walked back to his car in a tangle of sleds and bicycles, but the afternoon produced memories only of a half-renovated barn that had used up too much money too fast, and a couple of uninspiring nineteenth-century versions with sawed, not hewn, timbers. Perhaps I should call the angry divorcees again.

But a few days later the Barnmover called me: seems there was this fella down the road, wanted one of his barns down. Care to take a gander?

The farm was just off the north-south route from the Housatonic Valley to Vermont, on a narrow, flat plain between imposing, wooded hills. I suppose the road has been straightened and graded many times since those first woodsmen came over the ridge, hacking a trail through forests of huge maple, chestnut, American beech, yellow birch, occasional oak, perhaps commissioned to find a likely place for a stockade. That would have been after the so-called Deerfield Massacre when the settlements of the Connecticut valley were perceived to be in real danger from French and Indians to the north. Fort Massachusetts, manned by a couple of dozen military men sitting in the middle of a wilderness stretching for several-days' journey in any direction, made everyone feel safer in those days of polite warfare. In 1745 the fort was lost briefly to an invading force, but the French could find no use for it and left shortly thereafter. The fertile valley a few hours' ride to the west and south was settled soon after the end of the French-Indian wars, in the third division of land among the founding members of that township.

The house itself sat close to the curving, open road: modestly gingerbreaded porch, white paint, green shutters, comfortable, kept-up. Around back, the barns sat just on the edge of the valley floor, pasture land rising sharply behind them. The smaller of the two looked in good shape as we approached it. The other was at a right angle to it, with a cavernous wagon shed at ground level still crammed with farm equipment. The posts here were knock-kneed, the girder that supported the barn above, bowed and fragile; it looked as if it were on its way down, all right or, having lasted the winter with difficulty, was only partly alive, the whole caught in some sort of internal equilibrium unlike anything ever engineered by man.

My friend said: "That's the new one there. Ain't much

good." The older, smaller barn stood square, distinguished despite clapboards that were paper-thin. Along the foundation some of the exterior had rotted off completely, so that we glimpsed a part of its aristocratic skeleton. But on the whole it was a plain geometrical figure with pleasing proportions—a poor but genteel old English gent, clean white shirt badly frayed at the collar and cuffs. We pushed through a plank door that hung on one bent hinge, into the old stalls. At some point the barn had been given a concrete foundation and floor; some of the posts along the north wall had been cut off—the foundation wall was two or three feet high as a result, a common way to combat rot. Up a ladder to the loft we found the soft light I'd come to expect, rafters close overhead, the one bad place where that dormer had been stuck on. The beams were lovable, strong, not heavy, even the small knee-braces were hand-split oak, though no more than $3'' \times 4''$ and six feet long.

There are four bents to this barn: It measures $40' \times 27'$ overall, and is peculiar in its framing. The eight major posts are flared (as in almost all barns built before 1800) and support a truss that, from the look of the joint where post, wall-plate and principal rafter fit together was surely manufactured on the ground before the whole section was raised with pike and derrick. (It was the much more usual practice to attach the rafters *after* the perpendicular timbers were in place and braced.) The knee-braces that stand out so nicely are in place of queen posts, but this got the framer of this sure structure in a bit of trouble. The three bays measure (roughly) 16,

12 1/2 and 11 feet in width. The distance from the roof ridge to the wall-plate is some 21 feet, too long a span for the common rafters without some horizontal supporting timber. So a purlin was placed between the principal rafters in each bent. Again the span was longish: 16 feet in the largest bay. So the purlins are approximately $5'' \times 7''$, in turn too large to hang suspended forever by their tenons over that long span. So they have sagged considerably. The roof line is correspondingly wavy; charming, I hope, but just a bit disconcerting too.

I have a feeling the framer was a little too clever, perhaps more amateur than most, maybe trying an idea someone else picked up—a deviation that, once tried, was not to be tried again. (If the framer had included a queen post in his design, the purlin in question could have been braced diagonally a good four or five feet down its length, thus shortening the span and making it possible to use a timber of more manageable dimensions.)

As to dates, my guess is about 1763 to 1766. It is unlikely that the barn would have been built that far from the (fortified) town prior to the Peace of Paris, at which time the woods were finally thought to be secure from attack by native guerrillas. And it is unlikely that the builder would have gone to the trouble of hand-splitting the smaller braces if he had ready access to a mill. We know that one such was working by 1766, possibly a few years earlier. He may, of course, have had nothing to trade and/or been too cash-poor to use the sawyer's services; if that were the case we'd still have to conclude that the barn would not have been framed in the way it is later than 1766.

I wonder why it matters? The soft light now filtering through the fall afternoon makes a mosaic on the floor. The dust from two centuries of hay hangs in the air. Or does it? Is the light refracted in some different way by two hundred years of threshing, haying, birthing? Does each year make a lasting difference that we can, despite our dulled sensibilities, respond to? An antique dealer would say so, and then sell you a fake. (One thing is: it would be hard to fake an eighteenth-century barn.) I don't really care whether it's 1760 or 1800, I say to myself. But it's not true. Age itself has some value: survival, an extension beyond human life span, beyond possible human experience. I try not to guess how long it will live beyond me.

But I've not done justice to the way the place looked on that first raw visit. Here are some pictures. Clapboards peeling like dry skin. Over a side door a board is nailed primitively to the lintel, mysterious unless it was meant to be a drip edge. Vines on the north wall, a tangle of blackberry and whatever, the siding here dropping away in soggy handfuls. A ladder leading up to the open hay-loft door. I remember now almost falling, the ladder sliding about in the March mud and ice. The strange memory for me is realizing how much I didn't know, how differently I looked at this thing through my innocent and ignorant eyes.

In the original design the middle bay was left for coming and going. The milk herd lived in the larger right-hand bay, the horses in the left; headroom of not more than seven feet or so. The floor above both end bays was placed so that the major crossbeams, the ones that form the bottom of the roof trusses, were about three feet off the floor—waist-high, in other words. There was no permanent floor over the middle part, but the crossbeams had been mortised so that joists could be laid in if a bumper crop required more storage. The hay wagon would drive right in the middle bay, the hay pitched off into the lofts on both sides. Not knowing any of this at the time, I made no investigation of the dimensions, did not try to dope out how and when the main door had been altered (so doing I would have found out the probable age of the other barn, among other things). And as a further result I made some bad decisions, like how long the posts were going to be, since they had to be cut on account of rot; but more of this later.

I ran around it like a kid let loose in a toy store; it had a good feeling—modest, solid. I wanted it to be the right place, and knew that and stood back aways from the building to see if I was overlooking something dreadful. My friend said that it was a dandy, and—cleverly adding a pinch of blackmail—it sure was providential that I came along just then, because this guy was going to have it bulldozed or something, right quick. As we walked around cataloguing pros and cons he would say: "She's an old one anyhow, and not too big . . ."

I could see now that trying to move and make habitable that larger barn was labor on a scale I had not fully appreciated. I had been—still was—in a position to go right off the deep end; that I didn't was largely due to the good counsel of the expert. I was green and ripe, an unenviable combination, and to make it that much worse, I knew it. Almost unconsciously I looked for contradictions in the expert's testimony. I listened carefully, keeping my wits about me as my father often had suggested, trying not to let my need get in the way of my ears, my judgment. I needn't have worried.

I thought about the proud English barn, bought some graph paper and saw that it was both too small and too big and said yes. The reasoning was twofold: 1) nothing would be gained by looking farther, as my appalling ignorance would continue until I had actually gotten to work; 2) I was as sure of *my* eye for the old and the venerable as the Barnmover was of *his,* and I could see that this barn was old and venerable, perhaps even more than he suspected! (Thus the lure of the bargain.)

Still, it wasn't much of a decision. Anyone could tell, just by the way the building sat there, by the warm hard-used brown of its exterior, the pitch of the roof, the brave square corners, that this was a place meant to live on in some capacity. There was no mistaking it.

III

Trouble in the Pace

So an earthly match was made, and the number of possible alternatives narrowed to a manageable coefficient. Here was a piece of God's Earth, solid, granite-floored; in that next valley was the making of a house, ready to be picked-up, re-pegged, fitted out with sunlight and shadow, sounds of laughter, music, hot running water.

I went about telling people in properly hushed, self-conscious tones that I was, or soon would be, building a house. The future remained a blank, however. One foot in front of the other: I had started out on this journey a pedestrian very much on purpose, wanting to be intimate with all the details of the road, every stone and stump, to let nothing pass unnoticed or unused. But then the road had turned into an unmarked path, and the path had simply come to an end. I mean, the pleasures of that fine view, those hills against the westering sun, were quickly erased by a sense that I had no idea where to go next. In the city I woke up in the middle of the night wondering what was wrong, and remembering, felt my nervous system trip its fuse. It seemed plausible that I should hire some people to do this job, or at least a good part of it. Not necessarily the physical labor, but the planning, the logistics, the knowing of the order of things. I would be a benevolent overseer. I couldn't afford it, of course, but the bank could and even (so the argument went) would be rather more inclined to back the project if it had some professional standing. Then I could support the mortgage by renting the place and working at my profession: how uneconomic it is to waste time being an amateur—double losses.

But I know what an experienced craftsman says about the boss behind the boss's back, the implication always being that if only the guys with notions to match their bloated salaries would leave it to the working man the job at hand would get done better, faster—wouldn't cost 'n arm-'n'a-leg neither. Class, class-consciousness. My father's father was a furniture maker, much out of work, the victim of financial panics, stock manipulations in far-off parts of the world. The third generation would rather struggle than try to argue through the barriers created by a generation of upward mobility and "education." Because my sense of it is that the man with the plough, and the man with the hammer and saw, is right. He has for instance given us one of the few truly American ar-

chitectural forms, much revered in real estate sections:
the Cape Cod, the Salt Box, the basic New England
frame house. I do not have sufficient confidence in my
own vision to overcome the sense that the professional,
the craftsman, knowing more than I, cannot be given
orders, even though experience has shown me that prac-
titioners often get stuck in their ways. ("The hand that
knows his business won't be told/To do work better or
faster—those two things."—Robert Frost) Thus if I
wanted it done my way there was no escaping doing it
myself.

With that in mind I called the only expert I knew. I
hoped by this time that I was something more than a
customer. But he had treated me to an unusually varied
set of stories about city slickers and their foolish ways,
and I wasn't sure.

It was a bright cold day in early April, almost spring.
The children had come up for the weekend and we had
stayed in a motel, thinking that perhaps this time we
would find a more or less permanent place for the tent
and settle in. There still were isolated patches of snow in
the evergreen woods, like old newspapers piled up by a
capricious wind. The Expert arrived in a huge truck,
shirt-sleeved, quick and hearty. It was plain that for him
the spring had arrived: he had discarded the plaid jacket
that was his winter concession to the latitudes he lived in.
We climbed up the old driveway, muddy in the slanting
sun, past the foundation of the house that had so fortui-
tously burned. At the top of the rise I stopped, sweeping
my arm expansively at the stretch of field and woods, the

ridge across the intervale looking like a stage drop. I had talked to him about the land, describing it as best I could without overemphasizing those elements which mayhap I valued uniquely; now I waited for his appraisal.

He nodded. "Nice spot." A long pause. "Got yourself a real place."

Did I say it was a lovely morning? The earth was drinking up the sun, cooking. On close look—but very close—a tincture of green in the maple trees.

I had already cleaned out some of the overgrowth around the old barn site, revealing just a corner of stone retaining wall; it could as easily have been a terrace of some sort if we had been in another part of the world. I had thought to build there. I would dig a trench in back of the old wall, pour some concrete in it, and have a firm foundation that would have all the attributes of old and new. Would it work?

The Expert was patient, but there were so many things wrong with this idea that I immediately suspicioned he was in the process of concocting still another cautionary tale, one in the series I had been treated to over the previous months. Why does it strengthen our resolve to cluck over other bumblers' miseries? Or is it that the storyteller so shakes our confidence that we lose the thread of our self-interest, and the ability to perform the simplest sort of arithmetic?

His stories were told so artlessly!

Well, now, he would say, I had this fellow once, he wanted to put up this old barn I found him. Don't know how he talked himself into it (he smiles just slightly). Rot all round the edges, you know, and I thought well, Christ, I oughtta go up to this place, see where he plans to set up after I get it all down and laid out—that's if it don't come to pieces in my hands, you know. Sattidy morning it was and he comes up from New York, kids all around, musta stayed in a motel (Christ, cost him a fortune, didn't it?) and he shows me where he wants to put his house. Well, some don't have the sense God gave a titmouse, let me tell you . . . Had some idea he was jist gonna sit it down on a couple of stones in the middle of the field; sasif it was some kind of corncrib, barn with posts big around as your waist . . .

Reality infiltrates slowly. There was nothing wrong with my idea beyond the following: I had only about a half-inch tolerance on each dimension of the foundation if the frame was to be seated properly, neatly, for all time. Stones move around, which sure as spring rain you're gonna find out. It would be impossible anyhow to shore up that old pile of rocks less I wanted to dig it all out and rebuild the wall with mortar. And of course you wanted a cellar anyways. And how could you move a piece of equipment inside that wall there? And look, in case I hadn't noticed, it got cold around here; any foundation meant to last had to have footings three feet or so below grade. (Below *what?*)

Cellars. I've never much liked them. Digging down into the earth seems inefficient compared with building up into the air; I mean, air is a lot easier to displace. But it isn't like that, you see. Equipment, meaning back-hoe or bulldozer, can move a lot of earth mighty quickly, as

I *was* to find out; and in fact—any moderately knowl-edgeable home-owner probably knows this—it is one of the cheapest ways to create living space. A hole in the ground dug by machine, lined with poured concrete, costs a third to a quarter as much per square foot as space defined by wooden framing and sheathing.

Why hadn't I thought of that? I had been careful to mention my plan in the most tentative terms. I knew it would be unconventional and had prepared complicated arguments in its favor. In the event, it seemed smarter to keep quiet.

We started tramping through the overgrowth along the brow of the hill, my second choice in house sites. The Barnman liked it. He said: "One place I did, you know, the guy had a hilltop like this, he kinda set the barn off the edge so's he had family room down underneath." I wasn't sure I understood, but he got out a bit of pencil and a scrap of paper and drew me an explanation. I saw; it was like his own place. Yeah, that was it. The front end sticking into the hill, using the natural slope to create height in the back. It took me a while to get it (I'm not too good at abstract spatial relationships) because that would turn the barn 180 degrees, to a north-south rather than an east-west orientation. I had wanted the long side to face south, down the hill. On the other hand, this way the longer dimension would catch the afternoon sun. It would require some thought. In the meantime I wanted to show him the brook.

The wet leaves under the big beeches at the old fence line gave up a delicious smell of growth as our feet

TROUBLE IN THE PACE

ruffled through them. Fresh like yeast soaking in warm water, wafting up to us alone. Then the cold held in by the evergreens, a wetness that made me sorry I had not waterproofed my boots. The Barnman marched on. I had a feeling of elation, as if I had safely gotten through a difficult visit to the dentist: irrationally I had dreaded this meeting, afraid that neither site would be seen to be desirable to the one man whose cooperation I needed badly. But it had gone well. I would even use his suggestion, if only to put his mind at rest on the question of my good judgment. In any case he was a man who knew very much what he was doing, that was obvious, even in the way he strode through the woods.

We broke out of the spruce thicket into the open, beaver-cleared land around the stream, the sun so bright it was almost a physical shock. We walked quietly along the stream. Full of the spring runoff the water coursed over the banks it had worn itself, through a marsh that had once been a pond, then dashed on into the woods again. Here the stream is a good eighteen inches deep, smooth surfaced, not more than a yard wide.

Walking ahead of the others, the Barnman and I both saw a small brown trout reveal itself by dashing under an overhang. He started rolling up his sleeves, asking if I had ever caught a brookie by hand. No? Watch, he said, but keep back. With great stealth he lowered himself into the dry grass, knees underneath him. He had a bicep the shape of a large acorn squash. His face pressed against the brown grasses; he slowly sank his arm into the ice water. We could see that he was feeling under the bank. He spoke as a doctor to a nurse in a crowded ward.

"They stay still if they don't see you. They'll try to take a bite outa your fingers."

We watched. He waited, presumably making grubs out of his fingers, ready for that moment of supreme coordination when the hand would feel the trout's curious presence and snap it up by the gills. But time passed, as it often does. I wanted very much to see it work: a quick explosion of water and a shocked brookie flopping in the grass. What a sly, prestigious trick to learn. Just a minute, I would say, I'll just go down to the stream and pluck out a couple of trout for our breakfast. My friends would tell their friends that I had the quickest hands this side of the Allagash . . .

But not this time. The Expert gave it up, reluctantly coming to his feet, the bait still attached to an arm bright red with the cold. I guessed that it takes a while to psych them out. He agreed. This wasn't the best time of year.

Bears do it, Indians did it; still, I've never heard since of anyone who has actually managed such a feat. Perhaps it would be a little easier if you weren't looking for the one fish big enough to see in a quarter mile of rushing water.

Before he left, my friend had another piece of advice: dig several holes just uphill of the proposed site to see if they fill with water. This seemed a good idea: test holes. I had heard of that somewhere, but whether in connection with oil-drilling or ballistic missile sites I couldn't remember. Still, it sounded proper; and even if the expert was smarting from his unsuccessful demonstration of woodlore, it was unkind to think that he so needed to reestablish his standing that he would pass on otherwise worthless advice.

Later that weekend I spent some time with my only tool, digging into that rocky red soil. A shovel is not a good tool to make holes with, as any foot soldier knows. I spent a good deal of that time on my knees, then stomach, using my hands. I didn't seem to get down very far; the rocks kept getting bigger and bigger. A couple of times I was only a foot or so into the earth before I would hit something that was too big to move. Still, it felt good to get into the cold, sometimes wet grit and glacial debris.

The deepest hole turned up some reddish soil, rocks that fell apart in the hand before it bottomed out (as they say). We went back to look into its mysterious darkness later in the afternoon, one impatient adult and four smaller people in various stages of boredom, chill and disinterest, standing over a hole in the ground, peering blindly. Well, yes, it seemed that the wetness had accumulated, and the hole was *filling with water.* A miracle! But when I thought about it a little more, a tragedy perhaps? I ran for the shovel hidden under some young spruce. "Come on, Daddy," they said, as I sank once again to my knees, rolling up my sleeve, ready to explore that mystery, my face pressed to the ground in imitation of the expert. It wasn't water exactly. It was mud though. I would have to get the Man to come again. In the meantime we had to start the journey back to toilets and refrigerators, leaving the earth wounded and bleeding.

Having given the Expert the news on the phone, I

found him there the next Saturday morning before me. Together we poked at the hole with an old iron bedpost picked up from one of many dumps scattered along the back of the hill. It seemed to have less water in it than before. The post hit bottom with that uncompromising, solid sound that I later got to know well.

"Ledge," he said. "Shoulda known." The other holes similarly showed how shallow the dirt lay on the granite. As an afterthought we walked out into the field. He stomped on an outcropping of rock. "Yeah," he said. "Here it is again." We looked thoughtfully back into the trees, the way the land fell away from the hilltop. "You can tell, there's rock all under this hill. Better get yourself a probing bar and test out the whole area."

"How bad is it?"

Well, I'd find out sooner or later, but granite ledge isn't a bad thing to build a house on. On the other hand, it doesn't easily give way to man's design.

Anxiety, catastrophic expectation came in waves. I went in search of the required probing bar that afternoon, not knowing what such a thing looked like but confident it wasn't a tool that surprises you by its shape. The expert had said that they were expensive, and that if he were me he would borrow one from somebody. Now, borrowing tools is to be approached with extreme caution, as everybody knows.But since it also seemed the right sort of errand on which to make the symbolic connection with the town that had, sometime, to be made, I went down into the local communications center, the general store.

At one time, just after the railroad from Springfield came through in the 1840's, this town had two hardware stores of its own, and a store specializing in paints and varnishes, several factories making woven wooden baskets of the kind that were in use every wash day throughout New England, a silk mill, a mill making wooden dishes and, before the hemlock gave out, a tannery. Now the freight train doesn't even stop here, and people whisk through the town center stretching along the main highway before they know they're in it. (I did myself on that first trip down a twisting two-lane, following a good-sized brook. There suddenly was a church and rather a pleasing group of houses. But by the time I had said what's that, and the map had been gotten out, we were in the next township—really.)

The first town was organized around a lake. I suppose the water became a kind of common, providing good, easy communications. As the forest fell to the settlers, revealing the contours of the land, the hills beyond, it would have been a spectacular setting. Now that lake is edged with cottages two, three deep in some places, and the forests have regrouped. Only the most careful reading of the landscape reveals a few remaining details of that master plan. Medieval ruins are easier to read. Later the town shifted eastward to an important crossroads. But as soon as the railroad came through, the smart businessmen of the town picked up their enterprises and hauled them at a gallop to the shelter of the station ten miles to the east. Within a few years the former town center—inn, stores, churches—was as moribund as the stagecoach. Now it has been completely obliterated by a highway, as lost as if a rain forest had swallowed it whole.

This was never a fashionable summer or tourist spot, although there was an inn where the school now squats, and a kind of promenade along a plunging stream. Assistant bank managers brought their wives for a week in August, I suspect, coming and going via the Boston and Albany railroad from Springfield, Hartford, maybe even Boston itself. Then there was a flood, a war; the farms never were much. In the early 1950's land was bought for back taxes pretty near, twenty dollars an acre or less, owners desperate to unload a liability left by the careless dead.

I introduced myself at the store as the purchaser of the old Grimace place up there on the hill. I had been in the store before, of course, but anonymously, I thought. I didn't know what sort of information was stored amongst the cans of soup and peaches, hunting caps, fishing gear, greeting cards leaning heavily toward the beautification of Mother; surely it had the outward signs of the most effective of listening-posts. The Goodman listened to me as if he had either already committed my dossier to memory and found it uninteresting, or was waiting for me to make some egregious error that would quickly seal my fate. Perhaps both. In fact he did not answer the query at all, but was relieved of my oblique scrutiny when another citizen suggested I try the garage down the street.

I was looking for something I had never seen, in order

to poke it into the ground to see how thick that ground might be. It felt foolish. It was conceivable that I was looking for a left-handed monkey-wrench. It would be a swell story for the Expert all right; and if he did not have the malevolence of the compleat practical joker, circumspection was still indicated. A good mechanic is a pillar of the community by definition; it would not do to be perceived a fool. I drove slowly, in rehearsal.

But here is a man younger than I, whose handsome and equally competent partner is female. By their bearing you see immediately that both take seriously their chosen task—to keep the wheels of the community on the road. A hand-written sign hangs on one of the pumps: "NO CREDIT CARDS." *There's* a sign that gives one confidence; no pandering to international oil cartels here, it says. And, in the studied mastery of internal combustion machines, no room for nonsense.

I had bought the old Grimace place and would be putting up a house. I needed some sort of iron bar to test the ledge. All granite up there, you know. Impatient as any man interrupted at something he finds both interesting and important, he suggested I look around back, take anything that would do the job. Generally he tried not to lend tools, they have a way of not coming back, if I knew what he meant. Humbly I started looking among the familiar rusted debris of our mechanical age. But then the female side of the partnership came out to say that they had the thing itself at home.

Once I had it in hand I realized why I had bothered. A heavy, narrow, sharp piece of steel, five feet long.

Raise it up over your head, thrust it into the ground, rock it back and forth, draw it out and try to hit the same hole again. Unless it hits a very solid sort of rock it can bury itself in two, three tries. Compare this to using a shovel, to digging through that much hard, rocky soil in a couple of dozen different places. *Wham, thump*—good sound. Raising it, my eye was on the sparrow, bringing it down, I was feeling for the center of the earth. *Thunk?* The first time I wasn't sure and tried again. *Thunk.* Then another spot a couple of yards away. *Thunk.* In some places along the brow of the hill I got the *thunk* (though just a little higher in tone) on the first thrust. I worked away, drawing a diagram of the ledge in my head. There was less than six inches of dirt near the old barn foundations. Out front in the open field there was a bottomless pocket. Going farther into the field I realized that the outcroppings of rock all through it were further evidence of the ledge. But how obvious.

The while this was happening, we had been making camp at the top of the hill, convenient to transport and the well that had supplied the original farmhouse. On those first cold nights, frost would form on the inside of the tent. It was fine to wake to a gentle snow as the sun warmed the tent, the flakes just visible as they fell through impacted sunlight; then stumble to the edge of the well, the cold, clearest water bringing another day irrevocably into focus. (The water level was not more than a few *inches* below the ground, a bottomless gift.)

It was a convenient campsite but vulnerable. An automobile coming down the road would be upon us before adequate defensive postures could be assumed. Perhaps we should have a permit to light an open fire? Or park on the road. Would the tent be ransacked while we worked elsewhere? Best to remove your idiosyncracies from public view.

There was another, shallow well in the northwest corner of the field, hidden from the road by the crest of the hill. (To get it straight for once, the field slopes south. From the house site, looking down, it's about 1,300 feet to the fence line at the bottom. At the top of the field you climb from the road to the house site, then descend sharply to the evergreens.) We moved. Just in front of the row of half-submerged stones that marked the boundary line, we cleared a place in the young maple and birch—the picket line of the encroaching forest. We pulled up the small stumps by hand after axeing out as much root as could be seen. (Not the way to treat any respectable cutting edge, I can tell you.) Up went the umbrella tent and an auxiliary two-man pup tent. A fireplace was made near the well from the stones of the wall. Even someone coming over the brow of the hill would not see us right away. It was home: protected, free of anyone else's regulations; a campsite almost as neat as the illustration on the box.

Collecting firewood in the last light of that day, we tramped across the field to drag back another branch of dead, dry apple. A simple, ancient pleasure. The first stars in the east. Sweet smell of burning apple, the fire a fixed point in a changing landscape. Going and returning; a deep quiet, a truck somewhere or the insistent whine of a chainsaw. (Still too early for bird song.) The day finished. It was hard to see the twisting path we'd made through the saplings in the course of the remove, the path to the hearth, a going and returning. The fire became a beacon against the dark, deeper forest, a backdrop of extraordinary density, soft, absorbent, black. Some nanosecond between the going forth and slow return ("trouble in the pace and the uncertain/Wavering") the guarding spirits of this minute corner of our small planet gave me to know—at the very least, to hope—that it was going to be all right. Just that wavering moment dragging home firewood before the circle of light revealed hungry, expectant faces.

We were sparsely equipped otherwise. Plastic cups and plates, two hanging pots and a frying pan, food in cardboard boxes. We managed chicken grilled on the applewood fire; it had a pleasant sweetness (but you have to be careful not to let the fire smoke too much), potatoes roasted in the crevices of the stones and filled with butter: delicious. Even the raw vegetables were good; and coffee steeped in the smaller pot, ambrosia. (Why coffee is *always* best cooked next to an open fire is one of those culinary mysteries I want some day to solve.)

But eating that way, especially with your children around, needing to know they are not starving, may use more energy than the food one eventually takes in replenishes. I woke in the early morning hungry. We were all stretched out on the floor of the tent: wall-to-wall sleeping bags. Perhaps it wasn't hunger. Was it rain I heard or the wind in the trees? Please, my friend, no rain.

Perhaps I dozed, but now it was unmistakably raining. The longer I lay awake, the harder it came down. One of the girls sat bolt upright in her sleeping bag and said: "It's raining," and collapsed into sleep again before I had a chance to agree. I had tucked a poncho around the food, and the tent withstood the bombardment without apparent distress, but we had gone to bed late and tired; in the darkness it had not been possible to put things away properly. By daybreak it seemed a wise and responsible course to venture out into the no-man's-land, to look after our goods. I struggled into the other poncho. Outside, the fireplace was a basin of water, the remains of dinner scattered forlornly about. The box of foodstuffs had been partially exposed by the wind; water collected in the downhill corner. I stood there feeling my sneakers fill with water, wanting to run. (But not without the young'uns. I would wake them with cowboy shouts and herd them up the hill still in their night clothes. Hie, hie, get along there . . .) But no, last night we had been welcomed. Retreat wouldn't do.

Instead, using a plastic cup, I bailed out the fireplace. The cooking knife was just sharp enough to make some shavings; I gathered small sticks that had incidentally spent the night under the poncho. Inside the tent there were various paper burnables: pieces of a notebook, the jacket to a book on gardening. All of this I put into the dryer of one of the two food boxes (the food went into the tent), and shielded by the poncho, the fire miraculously burned, slowly, smokily. I hung the pot over it. Every once in a while as I watched the pot through smoked-glazed eyes, a figure would dash into the dripping morning to empty her bladder, a Chaplinesque routine.

The cardboard container of salt had not been put away. I poured some saline solution into the pot, plus a lot of damp oatmeal. I thought of Indians dropping heated rocks into their leather bowls, patient and accepting. By the time I had porridge made, the children were all sitting up in their sleeping bags, like so many fledglings: six empty mouths. We ate with plastic spoons out of green plastic cups. It was bland, glutinous; I passed around the saline solution. By now mud was forming on the floor of the tent from all the comings and goings. A box of sugar, not altogether dry, leaked its sticky contents. My stepdaughter decided that she couldn't hold out till the rain stopped after all, and went outside. Her oatmeal nonchalantly joined the bilge as she squeezed herself back into her alloted space, hair dripping. It seemed there was oatmeal between my toes. The rain began to work on the tent in earnest; the noise made it hard to think, or talk without screaming. Soon we were screaming.

My poor children. How patient they seem, after the event. Mostly they kept their sense of humor. Oatmeal took wings, voices reached into higher, perhaps near hysterical registers. Bickering finally broke out on the question of responsibility for the porridge now being ground into a good sleeping bag. The putative owner hadn't slept in it, but had spilled on it: should the owner clean it, or the borrower, who had had the night's use of it? It was a most unpromising argument. I found exile in the vast marshland around us preferable.

But what did we do with the rest of the day? Or was that the time we all showed up at the general store, and they wondered who we were, without asking? Was it the same day we drove to the Shaker Museum but it was closed? Did we spend the afternoon in rococo splendor watching a bad movie and nurturing a gigantic common headache? Never mind, the experience strengthened my (our?) resolve, and it was fine to know that the sky had fallen and we had survived.

In a late summer afternoon, having returned from a dunking down-stream where the water tumbles freely over the exposed backbone of this country, I read: "Near the end of March, 1845, I borrowed an axe and went down to the woods by Walden Pond . . ." He says later (by way of contrast to what you might just have read above): "It is difficult to begin without borrowing, but perhaps it is the most generous course thus to permit your fellow men to have an interest in your enterprise." Perhaps the arrogant young man is right, but it sounds like a rationalization to me. Then he adds: "I returned it sharper than I received it," thus giving proper New England respect to the material plane.

For my part I would not be without an axe. But then, I am twelve years older than the Preacher of Walden. My axe has lived for long periods under the seat of a car, or in the bottom of a closet with only a cast of dirty shirts for company. (I am still rankled by the "borrowed" above; Thoreau was living with his family in Concord in March of 1845, and I find it hard to believe that there was no decent axe somewhere amongst the Thoreaus' possessions. The more I think of it, the more I think he is cheating. That is, cheating us, playing loose with—can it still be said—Truth. It has spoiled this flamboyant sunset, crayon colors drawn all across the sky.)

The axe, a long-handled shovel, and a chainsaw were my tools. H.D., after borrowing "other tools" hewed his own rafters, floor timbers and studs "so that they were just as straight and stronger than sawed ones." On top of this he says, "Each stick was carefully mortised or tenoned by its stump." Thoreau must have had some talent as a woodsman, some knowledge of the method and means of turning his "arrowy white pines" into tolerable timber. He keeps this most interesting portion of his knowledge from us, however. It took him about six weeks to conclude this part of his experiment, although he didn't get to raising the structure, after digging a cellar and salvaging an Irishman's shanty for boards, until the beginning of May. He did so "with the help of some of my acquaintances, rather to improve so good an occasion for neighborliness than from any necessity." Here the braggart is over the hill. No doubt he *could* have done it himself with a series of derricks, pulleys, ropes belayed to stumps, but it would have been an altogether different and more difficult kind of operation. And his timbers were still oozing pitch, shrinking, warping as they dried (living white pine is on average some 62 per cent moisture, and his were cut well after the sap had been charmed up by the vernal sun).

I envy H.D. his time, his opportunity, the accuracy of his "narrow axe." He must have worked hard on the slopes above Walden Pond; he must also by that time have gathered a considerable array of tools: adze, broad axe, chisels, augers, tools that had been in use unchanged for a century or more, and the use of which was the currency of his time. And I imagine Thoreau in his bare study reconstructing Walden from notes, determining symbol from facts, making do with memory and a sense of having accomplished something important and tangible, something left behind.

In contrast, the chainsaw is my best neighbor. I took it and the axe up the hill one blowsy April morning shortly after the Oatmeal Disaster. I had two days to clear a site, or at least clear the ground where a shelter might go if you were inclined to build one. It wasn't a large step: saplings and undergrowth and an occasional scraggly spruce covered the top of the hill. I promised myself that if it began to seem like radical surgery I would content myself with cutting sight lines: that couldn't hurt.

But first, a latrine, a shit house. At dawn's light I began by digging a decent-sized trench between four small but sturdy birch trees, shielded on all sides by a grove of hemlock and far enough down the hill so that there was some soil on top of the rock. The birch trunks I notched about knee high, cut a couple of cherry trees in lengths long enough to span the trench longwise. These were flattened on one side with the axe and wedged into the notches on the living trees. Thus a two-rail shitter with lots of leafy material around to compost the rich refuse of our Arcadian repasts. It was accomplished before I knew it, a chore that would have been even more quickly done if I had remembered to bring some nails. (Nailing came later, but I hate having to go back to some piece of work, to have to keep in mind that this or the other thing has been left undone.) I had used a chainsaw before, indeed the moment of its arrival *in situ* was also the moment of its first angry cry of aggression. Still, this was the first real test of the machine over the smooth, flashing arc of my well-tempered axe and that sharp, attractive sound of steel cutting through the wood, chips exploding into the forest. Alas, the machine proved completely efficient despite its hideous whine, the awful danger of those hungry teeth whizzing around their track, eating away everything they happen to touch.

I use it under protest; its efficiency is tyrannical though it weighs hardly more than the axe, needs practically no maintenance other than simple periodic cleaning and sharpening. The whole thing is as terrible as the Industrial Revolution itself. Getting used to it is even more terrible. It is an uncompromising tool, overseer rather than comrade; treat it with the closeness other tools deserve, and before you know it the machine will make known its independence, taking away a piece of your anatomy in the bargain. But at the same time it is the essential tool, the thing I would require on that deserted island, the tool without which this enterprise would be impossible, or very nearly so. And H.D.T. would say that you had the Saint Vitus' Dance: "Why should we live in such a hurry and waste of life . . . When we are unhurried and wise, we perceive that only great and worthy things have a permanent and absolute existence . . ." (So, she says, he may have been smart but was he Happy?)

The work on the shitter proved to me, despite my conservative nature, that the chainsaw with all its difficulties was at that moment my most useful ally; even so it didn't do anything to improve a bad original design. I tested the throne just built. In case you take the account of this particular construction seriously, let me tell you that it is no improvement over the single rail. Evacuating while trying to span two logs doesn't work particularly well. A second log could serve as a kind of back rest, if you want; but the lowest latrine corporal in Caesar's legions knew the points of balance in the human body better than I.

Having made these momentous discoveries, and running on a chainsaw-induced high, it was time to get on with the first real work I had ever done on a permanent shelter of my own. In the meantime the sky had cleared. The field had turned its face to the morning sun: the site was roughly marked by stakes on three corners and a broken branch on a maple tree at the other. Is it necessary to say that, after repacing the boundaries, I felt like a nurse preparing to remove body hair? With some thought, and a sense of great daring, I tentatively cut a few saplings. How quickly the saw felled them, faster indeed than it takes to write down the words. But I stuck to the axe to trim the branches, dragging the brush out into the field, stacking the trunks—no more than poles really—between two silver birch. In this way I took out the major growth in the middle of what would some day be a house, perhaps. It went so quickly. Here was a tree that took five, perhaps even ten years to get here, and then it wasn't. The machine hurried me on. Soon I realized what a waste it was to put down one tool, pick up another, even though the sudden silence when the saw cut out was unalloyed pleasure. The rhythm was stoop, cut (close to the ground so that I wouldn't be taken for a novice woodsman), straighten, stoop, cut. Fuck it! After seeing what I had done, feeling gasoline rather than blood in my veins, I started in the upper northeast corner of my little lot and swept diagonally across it, taking down everything, the saw sweeping like death itself over the countryside, me hurrying to keep up with it, everything falling, plunging down in a heap as the machine spewed wood chips, me its slave stooped permanently in its train; roar, crash, roar. In that frenzy we cut over the whole lot, measuring about sixty by forty-five feet, except for two or three of the biggest trees, in an hour, perhaps an hour and a half. The small maple and ash and birch and cherry, the edging of sumac, the scraggly undergrowth I never did identify, all in a tangled mass.

Sweat was pouring down; I sought the shade lent by a few small evergreens on the fringe of the lot. (They too would have to go—I felt like cutting down everything in the county.) It was still only eleven or so. I had planned to be all day at this and perhaps the next; now it looked to be no more than a morning's work.

Sorting and pulling the brush into a pile in the field, stacking the logs took longer: there was a rhythm here, too, though it took a while to identify: it was complicated by syncopation, cross- and counter-rhythms. I used the axe, at first, but it's the wrong tool to use in a jumble of dying trees. The machine was what the song demanded, the rhythm was that of its internal, infernal combustion. I worked around the pile as if playing jackstraws. In another hour a huge stack of brush stood in the field, and the space between the two birches was filled with the trunks up to my waist. How pleased I was with the damage done. How different the landscape looked, truly like a newly shaven skull; what had seemed a gentle slope became a steep twisted hillside, altered *for good, forever.* For an antidote it was necessary to spend an hour sitting by the side of the stream, on a log easily a foot and a half thick, which ambitious beaver had gnawed down and trimmed with *their* amazing teeth, but which had turned out to be too large for their construction plans. A slight wind, that smell of evergreen in the sun, the hum of water moving over rocks.

Sobered, I spent the afternoon methodically cutting the larger trees, doing it by the book: cut a notch a third or more through the trunk, then cut through from the other side. The tree will fall using the notch as a hinge. So the mysterious skill of the accomplished woodsman, who can drop a tree exactly where it must fall, is quickly explained—and another childhood hero is unmasked.

I had been using the saw with such indiscriminate haste that I had cut through dirt, barbed wire, an old tin can. By early afternoon my impossible neighbor was complaining, cutting crookedly (the big maple was a challenge), and I was cross. For different reasons, we barely made it to the end of the job. Later I consulted the book. (It said: READ BEFORE USING on the front.) The cautions against misuse were very clear. The little teeth on the chain were no longer any sharper than a kitchen knife, some were bent and broken. Sharpen after every use, they say, and they're right. It's really a vulnerable tool, after all; like an indestructible twelve-year-old who's accident prone, it requires care—more than it seems to want.

Downhill from their stumps, lining the lower border of the new clearing, were a dozen or so good-sized logs. Thoreau: "So I went on some time cutting and hewing timber, and also studs and rafters, all with my narrow axe(?!), not having any communicable or scholar-like thoughts . . ." The tensile strength, the weight of those logs carried a seductive value, but time was short, I reminded myself. In any case I would not be doing any hewing that day: it was all I could do to stow the tools in their evergreen hideout, banking up the wet, old leaves to keep them from curious perhaps larcenous eyes. (But the precious chainsaw went into the car.)

I circled the clearing like a painter backing away from his easel. I would do a little more here, take that out over there. It had been a mindless, or should I say single-minded, entirely enjoyable day. *Entirely enjoyable.* I was ahead of schedule. For the first time I thought that in *actual fact* a house might finally rise from that patch, sheltering, comforting, resisting wind and rain and time.

IV

In the Exercise of Ingenuity and Contrivance

The next morning I crept up on the clearing cautiously, looking for deadfalls, errors of judgment. It was as if we had gotten too suddenly intimate the night before; tact was required to reestablish normal relations. Certainly that saw had run through a lot of living timber. In fact I would have liked to end the last chapter with a scene in which the ravager would stand on top of the hill, chainsaw still gripped in his hand (here an opportunity to allude to the slave/slave-driver symbiosis—the mutual embrace, etc.) and, overcome by the view of the distant hills or the sight of a purple crocus just pushing through the long abandoned flowerbed, would repent his destructive passion.

The truth is that the ravager had gone back down to the stream, taken off all his sweaty clothes and splashed about in the icy water, not daring actually to sit in it but doing the next best thing. At the campsite he cooked up a mess of baked beans on the gas burner bought "for emergencies," and, feeling lonely and purposeful, despite the usual ache in his lower back and a buzzing in the ears, fell early into a complete and blissful sleep. He was, after all, a day ahead of schedule. Time had been saved.

Saved for what, one might say, thinking of the Young Preacher sharpening his axe in the Concord woods. He suggests that if men could take time to construct "their dwellings with their own hands who knows but . . . the poetic faculty would be universally developed." Perhaps in our day, but we are already beyond redemption, Henry old son. I mean that any homesteader would be counted a half-wit if he were to go about clearing land with crosscut and a good narrow axe. Despite the fact that the saw requires a support system infinitely corrupt to human well-being, that its use is antisocial, capable of amazing damage to flesh and bone and the aural faculty, its saving in time and energy have made it the indispensable tool. Never mind the poisons that the machine farts into the air, there are many more exhausts being made to less purpose; as for the chain's havoc, we all lead charmed lives. And I am almost as proud of what I have been able to accomplish as I would be if I'd done it with less obnoxious help. Leastways I think so.

But still, we can envy those times when the source of suprahuman energy was an ecological asset, rather than a liability. And I wonder how much longer this job would have taken with sharp handtools and a mule to drag away the logs. Twice as long? Probably not, given the will to work and skills honed in childhood. (Don't tell me our choices are uncomplicated.)

In any case, I managed to accommodate my territorial ambition that manic April day, and the view of what had been done was not displeasing, after the first shock. Friends, including my wife, still thinking that I had lost my marbles, had told me that it would be prudent and in keeping with peasant custom the world over to build some sort of shelter near the contemplated site and watch a year go by, regarding the sun as its seasonal angles, the strength of the wind, the flow of ground water.

Yes. That would certainly be the way of an easy and patient mind; to sleep at various attitudes to true North at different times of the moon in different places, compare outlooks, the structure of one's dreams, work out some sort of equation that would give proper balance to these things as against accessibility to vehicular traffic, sun lines in summer and winter, condition of the subsoil, the water supply, etc. Books have been written on the subject. Indeed the Great Classic, Ramsey and Sleeper's *Architectural Graphic Standards,* suggests dozens of different tests on the subject of site orientation.

Okay, say I to myself in confident and manly tones: assume you've done the homework, all the algebra has been worked out, and the result is that the house should stand back there aways, where those maples are lined up, slightly east of south-southwest. You aren't going to believe it; you'll just flip the coin again. You can't know more than you feel, right? Just make sure you aren't overlooking something important. I had bought a dime-store compass: there's north; underneath is rock all over; over there is a well with water in it (barely a thirty-foot pull for the pump, although a couple of hundred feet laterally). Electricity was going to be a problem: the line would have to be buried if I wasn't to have lines stretched out across the view. But that was tomorrow's problem.

Maybe I was lucky; it fell into place. The gable end south, the long western exposure two-plus stories high, catching the winter's sun. The eastern (front) side would remain barn-like with minimal fenestration.

I had a ball of builder's twine (green) and a line level; I had to find out where the floor would be if I was to have a downstairs I could stand up in—harder than it sounds, really. I mean, the ledge slid downhill, then came back up again in a kind of ragged wave. Locate the high point of the granite and measure upwards from there, you say. It would have been easy with a surveyor's rod, if such came with a surveyor or just somebody with hands. Six feet, six inches I figured for headroom in the "basement" half of the downstairs, which would include the bathroom; the big bedroom, the space wanted for quiet, for a sense of separateness from the barn-room upstairs (just as the cattle stalls were nestled as close as possible into the ground), would be another step down, giving it sufficient height for its floor size ($15' \times 27'$).

So how do you do this without the proper tools or someone to hold the other end? Tie an end of twine to a maple tree at one corner approximately on a level with where the floor would be, walk down the hill with the other end, find that to get the twine anywhere near level you need a ladder. Instead of building same, toss the ball of twine over a convenient tree branch, tying it to a rock to keep it taut. Then cut a sapling seven feet six, allowing a foot for the footing (*that* seems right anyway), notch the end of it, and prop it up under the string, which (if only you'd tied a heavier rock to it, do that now) should hold the stick up if you haven't cut one too heavy (go do that again, cursing).

Then sit back and feel clever. 'Cause once one corner is fixed the rest can't be all that elusive . . . Of course, the downhill pole is too tall to stand without some help (rocks around its base), and as the line level has to be on the uphill end of the string to be read, it is thus probably inaccurate. I did a lot of running back and forth trying different heights for the downhill corner. (Cut yet another pole and measure it off with nicks.) There followed an hour or more of lower mathematics, none of which was really necessary but all of which felt good. It was a warm day; the May flies were beginning to come out. I sat with a pencil and a notebook figuring dimensions, getting up every once in a while to recheck something, digging down into the earth again to make sure I knew where the bottom was.

The result of this morning's research was to find that it wouldn't work. The house would have to be up on stilts if I wanted a basement. But that wasn't an altogether unattractive idea. If the house was set back from the brow of the hill some, dirt could be carted in to fill the resulting trench between the hilltop and the house, as if I had moved the top of the hill over to meet the foundation. That meant building retaining walls at both ends of the eventual house to keep back all that fill, but the idea of building some stout fieldstone walls was not unattractive either. How much would all that trucking coast? I had no idea—three hundred dollars, five hundred? The problem was more and more interesting as the options increased. How about setting the place at an angle, or like two boxes on top of each other but with a set back? How about moving the site altogether? The voices of the people who had inveighed against my haste came whispering back; what did I know about it? I moseyed about, poking the earth and tightening the guidelines. The more I thought about it, the less I knew. I was going to pay someone to pour a lot of cement on this hilltop, and then I would really be in for it. (Newspaper ad: "For sale, 48 acres, stream, views, unused concrete foundation . . .") Could a concrete truck get in here in the first place? I spent a summer once working for a mason: I could lay cement blocks. How many would I need? What about doing it right, using fieldstone? It would take forever, but there was the old house foundation by the road; would that supply enough stone? How would I get it from there to here? Rig a kind of sled, pull it with block and tackle? But I wanted some place to *be* in, for my children to be in; I wanted a house, not a hobby.

My father would tell me, keep it simple. Take one step at a time. ("Keep it simple." I wonder what he meant—

one thing, you make simpler mistakes.) Do it one step at a time. I'm not the first amateur who has tried to build a house. It's not even my first house. (The first?I was eight or nine. I decided to build a log cabin with my sister in the pine woods by the brook. We dragged a number of rotting pine logs into a rectangle: the walls were finished when the logs wouldn't stay one on top of the other. Later I argued for a doorway, and we stuck two crooked branches into the ground. It was only recently that the final traces of that perfect structure have disappeared, but I look for it still on every summer walk to the beach.)

My strings dangled there. Surely it was something funny that I was still doing the same thing, thirty-odd years later. Surely only an idiot or a genius would spend a day like this. I would either rent some surveying equipment, to do it all in a civilized, adult way or I wouldn't. In the meantime, enough.

Since the first inspection of the barn I had been back only once, to get a sense of how my fantasized plans would have to be revised to meet its specifications. That had been a typical amateur excursion—no proper notepaper, no one to hold the other end of the tape: all theory, no form. Think of trying to measure someone for a suit of clothes if you've never done it before, or even had it done. Where to start? What matters? I got some numbers on a piece of paper but they were completely meaningless: old lecture notes in a hasty, cold and near-illegible hand. The lines on that piece of paper had no relation to the picture I had first drawn of a house I would one day like to live in. A big space with several different things going on in it, all at once or serially. Two large brick fireplaces, one on each end, facing each other, laughing and dying at each other. One end would be for cooking and eating, the other for reading, thinking and talking (but damn little of the latter, as the Downeast Cap'n said to the First Mate). I wanted a tower too, when other things were done, with a skylight bathroom on top. Other sophistications abounded, none of them necessarily any less romantic. These misty plans defined my rose-covered cottage, my little grey home in the west; so far they had survived all challenges.

Still, the real world would require that I take stock of the limiting factors at hand. So at the next opportunity I went with my fourteen-year-old daughter to visit the barn again. A clear spring day. Warm out of the reaches of a fine, mocking north wind, that gentle reminder of winter's rigors. A cloudless sky of light blue: no leaves yet on the trees, yellow on the willows though, and a deepening color to the pastures.

Standing in the resolute clarity the barn seemed half naked. Cozying up to it, like some evil parasite, was the Barnmover's crane. Already he had got most of the roof off, exposing the rafters to the sun for the first time in over two hundred years. There was something particularly feminine and unsettling about the look of the place, and yet defiant too, as if it would resist to the last our attempt to retire it to secondary uses.

Sometime in the nineteenth century the original four

bays had been increased by the addition of one larger bay. That had already been demolished without ceremony, its parts lying about in gigantic disorder. But some care had been taken with the older part, as it seemed. The half-round minor rafters lay primly together on the wall-plate of the hayloft, leaving the four major trusses standing alone. (The Barnmover had said that he might try to keep the trusses intact, and move them as one piece—that is, as four pieces. It had never been done before, he said.)

Around the back the detritus from the roof had fallen on the tangle of vine and thorn that overgrew the foundation, for all the world like a trailing gown. We climbed through this mess and up the ladder to the hayloft floor, now obscenely bathed in sunlight. This was the makings of a house? Only an impractical visionary could accept such an idea without tremor, and my daughter was more than a little dismayed; where are we standing now? she would ask, looking for some geographical reality.

To me each joint, each nail was of interest. Here the roof boards must have pulled away from a rafter; there something with a wire handle had hung, perhaps forgotten for years. We could see the several histories etched into the shadings of the beams, just as you know where the previous tenant hung his pictures in a city apartment. Now those marks have mostly disappeared, and in their place are my fledgling memories of my house at different stages, history scratching out a few tentative new lines. It was bloody imposing to me, that weight of use. (The loft beams were rubbed golden by the comings and goings of centuries of hay.) Indeed as we clambered over the structure, like figures in a silent movie, I kept a narrow field of vision, not wanting to catch a glimpse of myself in the mirror of a world come apart.

To revive my memory, I have been looking at the photographs again, as Geo. Eastman knew I would. In one of these pictures you see the corner mouldings warping in the sun; the impulse is to reach for hammer and nails. Along the sill the siding has gone completely, exposing derma in even worse condition. Two small windows have all their panes, incongruously. And then there's the barn in the middle distance, some seventy-five yards away. I remember walking back into the field, wanting to record a sense of a place to come home to, thinking of all the times one farmer's son or another trudged home after the herd, or riding high on top of a load of hay slapped reins against a team of oxen. (Feel the hot, heavy afternoon air, sweat and dust, the sweet smell of the load, the task immensely important and uneventful. With luck the rain clouds building up there in the Northwest will hold off till evening; two more ticks to get in the old loft, and perhaps still time to ride down to the tavern, hear the latest news from the battlefields of Virginia— only that we don't whip 'em too quick . . .) It is almost real. It did happen that way. This is a real antiquity. But it's also true that there is no way we can know what it was like to have been that lad; too much is too different. We can only pretend to understand.

I turned the picture around, again making a house for tomorrow out of this shadow of the past. The most weathered side I could turn to the north, where it would be protected, like turning the collar on an old shirt. The south face would then be the side best preserved by virtue of its original location. It would stand thus for a while if the job were done properly, and I would honor it for the skill of its making and the volume of hay it had kept from the rain, accepting as is this fragile link to a valiant and difficult past.

I got out the tape measure and again tried to take down all possible dimensions: overall size, the distance between each bay, the girth of the posts, heights. But soon we were bogged down in contradictions. Measurements that should have been the same, weren't. Heights were hard to get; should we bother trying to move that ladder? It should be about ten feet from the roof ridge to the tie beam. What difference would it make if it were ten feet six? The picture of the barn I wanted was not after all to be found in a blueprint. It was out there in the sun-flecked field, minus the electricity lines, and I wouldn't see it even if I looked. It was gone, simply. I could commit my fantasies to paper as accurately and as purposefully without these figures. So, daughter/helper, let's forget it, again. It's no use. As the man said: Do it, don't think about it. Let's head back to camp.

Yes, we did accomplish something, though I'm not sure what: find some clarity that does not appear on that scrap of paper, that will not allow itself to be photographed or tape-measured. Fortunately no one else would need examine the report of the afternoon's expedition.

IN THE EXERCISE OF INGENUITY AND CONTRIVANCE

*　　　*　　　*

I was beginning to feel lost in a maze of possibilities, and as my attempts to extract myself through close attention to specifics wouldn't work, the only exit was—once again—straight ahead. Without further thought I would clean out the site: perhaps then the view would be clearer.

Of course H.D.T. did it all himself: "I dug my cellar in the side of the hill . . . six feet square by seven feet deep . . . It was but two hours work." You'll say I am envious of his strength and daring, his opportunity. He well may have dug such a hole in two hours, it's certainly possible in sandy soil if your hands are not given to blistering, you have borrowed a good sharp shovel, you are young and purposeful. On the other hand Henry's picture of himself in other parts of his writing is not compatible with this. His reputation in and around Concord, a community that surely put a premium on work, was that of a sometime layabout. Fair enough. I'm sure I would prefer the company of H.D. to that of Emerson or other Puritans of Concord, if I could be so lucky; at the same time, having spent quite a time with a shovel myself, I reject the idea that digging cellar holes is any more virtuous than planting a row of sunflowers, or even doing nothing on a brilliant spring day. And so would the Preacher. "I have traveled a good deal in Concord; and everywhere, in shops, and offices and fields, the inhabitants have appeared to me to be doing penance in a thousand different ways . . . The twelve labors of Hercules were trifling in comparison with those which my neighbors have undertaken; for they were only twelve, and had an end . . ." A good point, yes indeed. Vanity: the material world again forces entry. By our thoughts and by our deeds we sanctify ourselves in the eyes of our colleagues in the mode of our times. I wish only that H.D., Hero of my Youth, would not slip so easily into his own trap.

As for me, I thought of digging the hole with a good sharp shovel, but I didn't really think about it all that long. In any case the shovel is only the start: a lot more work would be done with a pick, as I had already found out. These Berkshire hills are still crumbling, of course; it is said that the fields in these towns have only one natural crop—stones. Pieces of the bed rock keep breaking off the granite, and because of the effect of water and changing temperatures, work their way to the top. Hence in a few tens of thousands of years, hundreds of thousands (what difference does it make?), the land could be flat as a pancake, but lined with the most fantastic stone walls.

I reckoned that if H.D. could dig his cellar hole in two hours, mine would take thirty-six, or three good long days attached to the handle of pick and shovel. Not too long when you think that it will *never have to be done again*. In the meantime you get to know the soil, quarry the rock. (There's that moment when a piece of the ancient granite loosens and you get an idea of how big or small it is—something like hauling in a fish.) And there's the treasures found everywhere just below the surface— plastic shoes, mustard bottles, evaporated milk cans, many small bottles of a particularly deep blue which must have been some kind of patent medicine, bits of complicated machinery.

I kept the option open and called a man who had been recommended. He was pleasant on the phone and the following Saturday morning appeared right on time in a shiny, new, red-and-white one-ton pickup with an extra row of yellow lights festooning the cab.

In a way this was the point of no return: once that bulldozer started to work, there would be no changes without extraordinary cost. He was a small, tidy man with busy hands. I welcomed him with mixed feelings. He looked over the site and wondered why I hadn't taken out more trees: he didn't know whether he'd have room to move around, but he would just buck out these maples here and over there on that side. Where would I want the stumps and all? I explained the results of my geodetic survey; I tried the amusing rather than the purely informative version of the story: he figured he'd get it all off, whatever. We walked over one of the piles of old trash, the ground springy from the volume of rotting tin cans just under the turf. He kicked at it: maybe you wanna cover this all up at the same time, only way . . . We walked back to his truck thoughtfully, me dreading the moment when money would have to be mentioned. He was interested in how he was going to get from the road to the site. Perhaps the thing to do was to put in a road here at the same time, need lotsa gravel for this hill, make the job easier, couldn't count on this bank holding.

Already this stranger had decimated the sugar bush

and sent a two-lane blacktop straight over the prospective flower bed. Yes, says the sheep thoughtfully, marching off to the slaughterhouse, yes, I suppose you're right: it would have to be done sometime, and sooner better than later. But (a little brighter now) there's this problem about money, that is, cash money. So leaving out the superhighway with the double clover-leaf interchange just for the moment, how much do you think, actually, in dollars and cents, for the basic work, I mean . . .

His ball-point came snappily to hand, a notebook was extracted from beside the tire-pressure gauge in the other shirt pocket. The Technocrat leaned over the fender of his admirable, spotless pickup and began to do some figuring. The pen clicked a couple of times in the ensuing silence. "Well, now" (he looked rather pleased and conciliatory) "it figures out to be—including the traveling time and all, all-inclusive, I mean—I figure I could do it for about" (with superb timing, he pauses a moment, leaving his audience on the edge of the pit, so to speak, if not on the edge of a heart attack, and glances down to pick up the cue from the Teleprompter) "about two-fifty."

Two hundred and fifty dollars? What was it that I had been expecting? Two hundred and fifty polished stones, my first edition of D. H. Lawrence, memories of hungry babies at two A.M.? As I waited to see what I felt about the idea of spending two hundred and fifty dollars on digging a hole, my impressively coached interlocutor said something to the effect that if we could come to some decision then and there he had some time in the coming week, a job postponed . . . Two hundred fifty buys you a good suit of clothes, a broken-down car that probably won't work for long, a table saw with attachments, and a cellar hole for a house that was going to last the rest of my life, maybe beyond.

I really wanted to say yes and get the whole thing out of my hands. But there was something about the gleam in his eye that made affirmation impossible. He would be here with his 'dozer while I was in the city working to pay him off; his vision of long, straight gradings, gentle banked turns, the civilized world as a series of fairways, would come with him. That sequence kept me from finding a mutually understandable sound for "Well, yes, I guess maybe under the following conditions." I tell my children that "no" is an efficient word in such situations, but for some reason I couldn't form my mouth around it. Looking for time, I said okay, *but* (inspired) I would have to find out where the money was coming from. I would call. And he said, Well, yes, that's okay, but call Monday 'cause things were gettin' busy, and he couldn't be sure he'd be able to get to it . . .

I felt pleased. There was reassurance to be had from the notion that I no longer had to worry about *whether* someone would do it, but only how much it would cost —a step very much in the right direction. Still, how much more satisfying in the end to have done it myself, with pick and shovel. Was it ridiculous? Was it more ridiculous to *hire* someone whose major expense, from what I had gathered, would be his transportation to the job? And—vital point—if I did it myself I wouldn't have to talk to any more technocrats. But I am probably the only person in the world to whom three days' hard labor has a discomfort rating about equal to a couple of telephone calls. I should try again.

My nearest neighbors are a theatrical couple who have been fixing up a one-time hunter's cabin on the other side of a massive, heavily wooded knoll to the south. They have a telephone. When I went there to look up another "EXCAVATING. BULLDOZER WORK. NO JOB TOO SMALL," they recommended someone who had done work for them. Would it be all right to call now, Sunday afternoon?

He was home, and yes, he knew the place. I explained the task: no problem, seeing he was goin' to be down by there doin' some work on the telephone line, he could get right at it. He got seventeen dollars an hour for the D–3, door to door. How long? Well, you never know, of course, but shouldn't be more'n a few hours. (A few equals five at the outside? Figure five times seventeen, which is half ten times seventeen, which had to be less than a hundred dollars. Hot damn.) What? Yes, I had cleared the site myself. Just at the top of the hill where the road drops down. (But wait a minute. Was I looking at something for nothing again? A cut-rate bulldozer goes zipping off through the field, tearing up blueberry bushes.)

Ah, I mean, well, if you could . . . I don't know but, ah, do you work on Sattidy? (Was the pronunciation right? Were my hosts looking at me kinda funny?) There was a moment's hesitation on the other end of the long copper wire. Was I still the weekend frontiersman, boots from L. L. Bean and overalls from Abercrombie & Fitch? The balance hovered, but the voice came back, readily agreeing to meet Sattidy mornin'.

We were all there the next weekend, eating our cereal as the morning sun crept through the grove of young maples, leaves like mouse's ears (time for plowin', they say), birds again making known their place, their pleasure, in the gathering spring. By that time we had had our fill of cereal flavored with the sweet, sticky taste of applewood; and as I was not then enough of a woodsman really to *see* the other dead wood we could have cut up for our fire, we used the efficient bottled-gas burner: the water boiled promptly, and the porridge seemed to appreciate the technological improvement. It had stopped raining every weekend, and we had worked some other things out: a bucket that could be put into the well for keeping milk and butter, and tin bowls, and a screw-top container for sugar. The process of acquiring a household's goods had begun.

It was early; we all had our ears tuned for the expected visitor, though when one of the kids asked me how a bulldozer gets to work in the morning, I couldn't say. And I was mostly sure it wouldn't in this case. Not being able to get in touch with us was the perfect reason for the 'dozer man to busy himself with something else instead. I would have to call him again, and he wouldn't be there. It would take several days. Then he would be booked solid for weeks. I controlled my catastrophic expectations with the idea that it would really be better after all to do it all by hand. The children could haul dirt away in baskets, like coolies working on the transcontinental railroad.

But we had not really finished our peculiar breakfast when we all heard the unmistakable sound of an airbrake, and then several more. It was all of seven thirty; I thought, the day had already cost me $8.50.

As we approached, the dozer was panting on its trailer, ready to get to work. The man putting the ramps in place was smallish, round. He wore glasses, and a fine, energetic smile came across his face when I introduced myself. He said, "I wondered if this was the place. It's not too good gettin' that thing goin' in the wrong lot." We laughed, realizing he recognized and would make allowances for our anxieties. He climbed up, and the machine took him politely, proudly through the field, conserving energy. He rode it with respect but also authority, like a good horseman or an elephant trainer, careful of the footing.

The Trainer left the Beast pawing the ground to have a look at the site. But he didn't want to contemplate the task at hand. He asked if I had a saw, and showed me what had to go. He hadn't room to turn around, and anyways the trees were growin' that close.

Again he anticipated me. I had taken the fading green string down, but the corner markers were still in place and they were enough for him. His first swath took the stumps out of the soil neatly and deposited them downhill.

Stumps went one way, the topsoil—what there is/was

of it—went another. The Beast was very good at what it did; there was exhilaration in working with it, clearing a path, felling and cutting whatever was in its way. Bucking along, the blade made waves of soil at its front, huge rocks rolled up like driftwood in ocean breakers.

My nearly grown-up children, wife and baby lined the clearing, cheering us on. The Trainer says people always do: the power of the Beast is mesmerizing, like fire. They had a small tape-recorder. Someone did a sidewalk interview: it is uncomfortably excited, as if the roar that you hear in the background is the *Hindenburg* in flames. Yes, and that is a real baby you hear, screaming, the mother being soothing and excited at the same time, full of questions and energy, and perhaps wounded at this abuse of Mother Earth.

But the gallery drifted off in a little while, and the work got harder. Before long the Beast's tracks began to slip, the ground was muddy and less forgiving. The Trainer stopped, dismounted, and knelt down to take a close look at the quality of my dirt. "Greasy," he said, and it was—a fine, wet, clayey mixture, chocolate brown in color. A couple more swaths, and the tracks began to spin and kick up sparks at the same time. The blade hitting the same ridge of granite complained in the same terms; I was not meant for this, it said.

The Trainer took another pass, gritting his teeth and shaking his head. He didn't have to tell me that the floor had been found. It took but another few minutes to scrape away the remaining loose dirt, or at least as much as the blade could get to. Then the Trainer put his Beast back in its trailer, and (to my surprise) said yes when asked if he would like a bowl of soup. We repaired to the campsite in the wood. A fire was going and a large pot bubbled away, aromatically.

He charged us for three hours work, not counting travel time, since he was comin' down this way anyhow. But I think he was influenced by my daughter's tomato soup—or a clear-eyed view of the enormous job ahead of us.

It seemed a giant hole; actually it was but three or four feet deep at the most, and on much of the downhill side, where the covering of soil was thinnest, it was barely two feet lower than ground level. The rock was exposed here and there in a sea of the greasy mud/clay mixture. It was hard to imagine a clean, dry house rising out of such a pit, even harder to imagine how it would fit into the landscape. What, for instance, would be the view from the living-room windows which would some day be hanging up there in the sky? I wouldn't know until I had done it. People make elaborate scale models of things, I remembered, every tree and eventual shrub in place, in order to get light, views, distances in proper relationship to each other. Or else they didn't care. At times like these blind courage must take the place of sense.

In December 1845 (coincidentally Thoreau's first December at Walden), from Lenox, Massachusetts, Samuel Gray Ward, a young man sent West for reasons of health, wrote to his father in Boston: "I love farming. There is such a variety and simplicity, such an adaptation of means to ends, such room for the exercise of ingenuity and contrivance, as well as for the cultivation of perseverance and patience . . ."

The day dawned hot. In the still-barren landscape it must have been 90 degrees Fahrenheit. Strange summer hotness in a land that seemed blighted, shadeless and unforgiving as the day grew older. But it was time, perhaps even past time, to get a garden plowed. I had chosen a fairly level patch on the sloping field in front. Where was my predecessor's garden? The first whiteman there, where did he think to start his corn and turnips and potatoes? In my past experience, the place to put a garden had been determined by the narrowness of the holding, or the proximity of a water supply. Thus, I had first thought to clear a patch near the well, worried about getting water to the veg in August. But that would have required cutting a lot of trees if the garden was to have morning sun. Also it seemed a good idea to be able to watch over the patch from the house, if there ever was going to be a house; and any book I had ever looked at emphasized sun and drainage. The field slopes south, is in constant sun, and the granite keeps the water moving under the surface.

We had rented a small, gas-driven tiller. The turf was stubborn; at first the tiller churned at it without doing any discernible damage, like going after a giant sequoia with a boy-scout hatchet. The job required all that morning, churning and bucking over that small rectangle of planet Earth, turning up bits of metal, tin cans that caught in the tiller's tines, a brass drawer-pull (which became the handle for the garden gate eventually), pieces of plastic toys, a rotted baseball, a length of chain, a light fixture.

The sun burned down out of a hazy sky. Sweat dripped across my glasses and off the end of my nose. There were clouds of black flies about; keeping thoroughly dressed was a necessity. Often I had to stop to cut the grass and vines off the tiller's axle, a chore that takes more skin off more knuckles than any other I know. There was nothing dry or clean to wipe my glasses on. Nevertheless, crouched down in front of that panting machine, in the newly turned soil with that damp, brown smell of riches in it, the discomforts of ground-breaking became a worthy, even joyous penance.

Later that morning I heard a truck stop in the road. Shortly a heavyset man came over the brow of the hill. I had seen his cows grazing. He excused his intrusion on the grounds of neighborly curiosity, looked over the field and remembered when it was sown with corn; he said he reckoned it was one of the best fields around.

Then he resettled his cap on his head, crossed his arms over his dark-green work shirt in the manner of a politician going on the record. "It'd be good to see somethin' growin' here again," he said. And I told him it was my purpose to see that happen. Then we talked of other things.

I have learned since that he is a part-time farmer, that his dairy herd is the only one left in town. (Curiously, his visit was also the only one I had from any of my neighbors. If they had any curiosity they satisfied it when I wasn't watching.)

By noon the soil was as cut up and mixed about as it was going to get. The plot was but twenty by forty: I dug a trench around the perimeter to bury the fencing, then the post holes.

In the stillness the mayflies were a constant menace, even the Trainer had said so. So many buzzed around your head that any quick movement, coupled with an intake of breath, would drag a couple into your mouth. (They taste all right, rather nutty, and I theorized that eating them is a possible antidote to the welts they can raise.) The heat was oppressive in the sun, even worse under the bare trees, where not the slightest breeze moved the tent's heavy green canvas with its heavy, bilious smell. The baby couldn't sleep; sweat poured off him, too; he cried—sleepy and uncomfortable. But to lay him down outside meant watching constantly for the flies, standing over him like a harem slave. We should go, really. In the middle of the day—in the middle of making a garden? I'm not enjoying this much either, you know. Reverse roles? Okay; you wrestle with these fucking posts. Well, she said, it's not fair. Yes, that's so—but life isn't fair.

What is it that is fair? But the question is itself explanatory, and cynically superior, a challenge. The post I was hugging to my chest resisted, came up against my chin: fury, retribution, awful frustration took its place. Fortunately the plowed soil made a reasonable good wrestling mat. She had the first fall, but I turned her and could have gone for the pin if I hadn't thought that I should not take full advantage of the fact that we were fighting out of our respective classes. We parted. I was taken down again, however, much to my surprise, and, realizing that I now had to use whatever advantage appeared, went in for a quick pin.

It was a silent fight, no cheering, no coaching, perhaps a mutter or two. But a wonderful eruption of violent language followed. How the air sang with our vilification, a blizzard of wretched curses flew through that hot Venutian landscape.

I was being asked to share more than I was prepared to share; I could not sacrifice the morning to babysitting; I did not have sufficient trust in the future in general or ours in particular, despite my last-born and only son (or because of him, thinking I knew where the required compromises would have brought us). By extension I could not change the singularity of my fantasy to suit another. If that is an error (and I believe it is) it is bred in bone.

Winded and feeling terrible, still angry, still thinking that what I was doing was for all of us as much as I could make it so, that indeed it was the best that I could do; wondering what it was that I was wanting to ferment such anger, I listened but didn't watch as the car loaded up, doors slammed. One voice said, Call the bluff; it's the only chance. The other said, Help, please, I don't want to be the stronger/the stranger. But the car started up, the gravel in the road scratching out a noise that said good-bye as it accelerated down the hill.

Two marriages, two failures. Still, the garden needed a fence, and the land would grow vegetables no matter what the state of my domestic life. I sat in the would-be garden on a hillside that seemed to my starving eye to

have something organically wrong with it. No shade anywhere, nothing growing. Blight, a plague of lovelessness
has captured my homestead, my refuge from old terrors'
continual cry, from the stupid brutality of crowds. The
land was sown with salt. No roots would take hold here.

Finally, I walked to the neighbors to see if they were
going back to the city or could take me to the bus station
fourteen miles away. They weren't. They were clearing
out their woods. Yes it was hot; tomorrow it would be
cold again. The flies were bad. There was always a day
like this in the early spring. (Like this?) I could call the
drugstore for the bus schedule and a taxi. I thought with
pleasure: No, I would hitchhike, as of old.

I took a shortcut through the woods, heading back to
the tent. No telling how long it would take to hitch. Bus
at five: I had time to make a sandwich, shut up camp, dip
myself in the stream and sit in the cool evergreen woods
for a bit. The woods were dark and quiet, the stream yet
too cold for total immersion. I watched the small fish, the
scooters, listening to the eternal sound of the water
pouring down to the sea, maintaining its circle, maintaining life. (If I peed into it here, how long before it would
reach the open Atlantic, the shores of Cape Cod? Down
the valley, through the town to the West Branch of the
river, into the Connecticut . . .)

It would be cold again tomorrow. It would rain. There
were killing frosts in May. It was important to plant, to
prune those old apple trees, to see somethin' growin' in
that field again. Without roots the soil would wash down
to the sea with my urine. And yes, it is necessary to insert

ourselves somewhere in the circle, in the striving for completeness.

I thought: Without her I could not have made it this far, that is true. But if we can no longer get on together, that need not be a contradiction.

And then I heard my name sounding through the woods and the hollow sound of my own reply, as if I had already grown unused to speaking. The self-pity could be put away; perhaps some patching up, some complotted scheme could still make it work.

V

Heading for the Barn

Bloody woodchuck has been eating the beans again. The first planting had been coming up nicely when he/she found a way into the garden. Nubs; all those fine, strong leaves making their way into the air. Gone. I found the burrow once, burned it out, replanted. But the bastard's still lurking about, watching every crack in the earth for newly sprouted delicacies. The peas have been half eaten, some of the cukes, half the squash.

Early this A.M., before the day had properly declared itself, I went down to the garden to see if I could catch him at it. No chuck, but it looked like further damage had been done to the cukes in the far corner. Logically the new home would be over there under the rotting apple trunk: they like to keep their supply lines short. Poke around in the blackberry briar. A surprisingly large mound of fresh dirt. Could it have been there yesterday? Anyway, she/he et al. got a cyanide bomb for breakfast.

Early that first summer I was surprised one morning to see a mother chuck lead her young out of a hole on the other end of the same sad relic of apple tree. She saw me right away and shooed her young back indoors. I thought then: I will take whatever precautions necessary so that this friendly, furry creature, whose field I am invading, can remain our neighbor. Later when I realized that my stout fencing provided only the merest touch of exercise for the ravenous family, I laboriously filled up the burrow, after giving them all a proper, even polite, eviction notice. That was before; now I am a householder myself. I am pleased with the probability that mother, father and offspring all were enjoying the comforts of home when the gas started coming out of the walls. I'm a law-and-order man, Mr. Chuck; this is the '70's.

We need rain, too. The soil is cracked and powdery on top. I would get out the hose but the hastening clouds have looked as if they were just about ready to dump on us these last couple of days. In the fullness of time there will be a barrel or two down there, filled with rainwater collected on the roof. In the meantime watering means running a hose some two hundred feet and listening to the damn pump turn itself on and off, remembering all those joints, valves, a plumbing system I know too well to be at ease with. Sooner or later something will break. Let it be later.

And let it rain for a while; let the water in the well rise, and the swampy patch at the top of the hill send its slow tide creeping along the granite, working down toward what remains of the garden veg. Let the miserable woodchucks rot beneficially in their burrow.

Yes, the outside trim has been finished in the meantime. It took better than a whole day in the event as I decided to caulk all the interstices, hanging over the edge of the roof and wishing I had taken the time to build a proper scaffold. It should be years before strands of resinous rainwater will again surprise us as we sit at table, and in half my mind I already miss that recurring proof that we are not really safe from erosion, eventual malfunction, premature death.

You can't just cut down trees and put up a little ol' log cabin these days, you know. Or even dig a hole and climb in. A building permit had been applied for in March. My first thought was that the lawyer ought to get that sort of paperwork off my hands, but he seemed disinclined to spend my money doing so, and I thank him for that. He suggested a letter to the Board of Selectmen.

In answer to my query I received a form. One page: name, location, type of building, lot dimensions. I was told that a Percolation Test was Required, also a Septic Field Inspection. But when, what order?

I returned the form and two weeks later was told that "Your application is in order," but no permit would be issued until "proof of a certified percolator test is received." There was a number to call. The Inspector gave me to believe that I shouldn't have anything to worry about. Of course you're on the top of the hill, he said, you never know. Dig a test hole.

I learned that a septic system is required in all new habitation by State Law; I would have one even if I didn't use it. Progressive legislation, I suppose, cleaning up the waterways. But what about the enormous waste of water and the energy needed to pump it? Whither the convenient and functional privy? An ecologically sound indoor, waterless toilet costs as much as my sewage system did (about six hundred dollars). Just now I can't afford to join in that interesting, water-saving experiment. Thus an enormously wasteful and expensive norm is established. It will be years again before the legislature can be brought around to consider a new point-of-view. Properly cared for, our excrement is excellent fertilizer; why is it unspeakable?

In my case I was worried about finding a place to put the damn thing. A concrete septic tank needs some six feet of soil; the law says there should be at least twenty-four inches of dirt over it. The sewage treats itself in the tank, separating, decomposing, settling. The runoff is distributed under the ground through fifty feet of porous tile sloping gently away from the tank—provided the soil is sufficiently absorbent, as determined by the percolation test.

If it is suggested that I dig a hole, well, it will be a good one. I spent an afternoon at it. My young son was entranced. He toddled about, playing in the growing mound of rocks and dirt. He liked the top, watching the dirt fall around him, a happy annoyance for me. But when the granite bottom was found it was still a couple of feet under regulations. Just right for a foxhole commanding the valley; I would have a wide field of fire. A Demolition Team would blow up those trees so that we could cover the road . . .

The man came on a Sunday with a bucket, a measuring stick and a watch. I had thought that a percolation test would chemically measure the moisture in the soil: a lab in the back of a van sprouting antennae, men in white coats. It had been raining and I was worried anyway, figuring this is one test you don't want to fail. The actual equipment suggested a procedure too simple to be inaccurate; should I be relieved or apprehensive?

I gave him a tour of the fortifications; I knew it was a good hole, albeit a mite shallow, but he wasn't interested. "You dig that?" he asked, as if it were some peculiar sort of recreation.

We went into the field. He bid me take out a shovelful of dirt here and there. It required three tries before we got a hole he liked. I poured well-water into it, he inserted his calibrated stick and checked his watch. Nothing seemed to be happening and I scrutinized his face for signs of disapproval. "How slow can it be?" I asked. Silence. I was sweating.

I asked again, my voice too loud. "Ah, I mean, is *anything happening?*" I waited.

He had his finger on the stopwatch, looked up. "This is fast for around here," he said. "Last place I was at took an hour an inch."

Fast? Terrific! What about the tank? Well, you can get

that in somewhere even if you have to hill up the dirt a little. (Why hadn't I thought of that? Too simple?)

Already he was filling out the form that gave me permission to Construct an Individual Sewage Disposal System. I filled out a check for twenty dollars; my troubles are over, I thought. Relief must have showed in my face. "Well," he said, "now your troubles begin, but fortunately they ain't in my department" But he smiled, faintly, as he picked up the tools of his Sunday trade.

The first three people I talked to about the foundation didn't even want to make me an estimate. One of them lost the way, never showed. The next took one look and said: "I don't think you're gointa get a cement truck up there; besides, you're gointa need special forms." He wouldn't have his forms all broken up. Maybe make special ones, but then he would have to charge me for *that* time and all, and key-riced it'd get expensive.

Was I being insulted again? So out of step as to be untouchable? To each his own, he said, but as for him he wouldn't take a job whereby he hadta break up his forms.

Who should I call? Surely it would be worth *someone*'s time. Well, if it was him he would think about getting someone to lay cement block: "There's lotsa guys do that sort of thing." (And there are others that have unspeakable social diseases, he seemed to be saying.)

I resorted to the local Yellow Pages. Two calls, and I found someone unbusy, who gave me the number of a man who he thought might take the job. He arrived on a motorcycle, helmeted and supercharged. He admired the property. He studied the wounded earth, the debris of this and previous settlements, as I explained the situation as best I could. He seemed to be listening to the call of the open road. When I finished he looked up: "See many bikes out here these days?"

I took a deep breath and asked him how much he would have to charge to make this job worthwhile. With difficulty he applied himself: He couldn't do it. Much easier to pour. Thing to do is ask Louie. He'd do it.

Louie's truck showed signs of having been worked hard. It was afternoon quitting time for him; I was happily cutting out sumac, further exposing the bit of tumbling stone wall. He was a man of small stature, but large and robust of spirit. That morning the green twine had gone back up, aiming the house roughly north with the help of the compass. He took notes, making no comment, occasionally asking for dimensions in a strong, unplaceable European accent. We took the steel tape to it, just to make sure. He calculated on the front of the same envelope. He would do it for $2,200. It could be done in two weeks. He was worried about getting the cement trucks up the old driveway. If it rained he would have to spread gravel. I would pay extra. Loaded, it don't take much to flip them trucks over. (Like a giant tortoise, I thought, never to be set right again.) We got good weather—he was working in the neighborhood anyways —he'd pour footings this week.

But he hadta know because things get busy. He did good work, I could ask anybody. No money paid till footings in, he know so much I like. Whaddaya say?

A clinching argument, no matter that he knew well its force! I countered by taking his hand on it, but also offering a small down payment to show my own good nature. His smile shone even brighter on a face built for smiling. It was done.

He glanced at his paper again. Reinforced corners? Oh, yes, naturally. Footings two feet wide, eight inches high. Windows? Oh, two please, in the east wall. Doors? (Think a little on that one.) No. No doors needed. I did need a footing running down the center of the building to carry the middle posts. He grimaced. Okay, he would do, no extra.

He was an experienced man; before he got into his trucks he cautioned me on any changes of plan. "More cement costs more dough," he said.

As he forced the truck into reverse, I noticed for the first time that there were two other men in the cab. They seemed to have been asleep; indeed they stirred only slightly as the truck stuttered backward. I guessed that Louie got a hundred per cent from his crew.

On the drive back to the city it seemed to me that the arrangement with Mr. Louie might be made a little more formal. Once poured out of these enormous, reptilian trucks, cement is hard to move. I would consult Ramsey and Sleeper. (A friend who is himself a practicing architect put me onto this famous compilation of ephemera. It was before I had really made the decision to do without professional guidance. In answer to the most obvious question, he replied: "I'd never hire an architect if I were you." Me: "But surely . . ." Architect: "Thing is, building an uncomfortable complicated house is exciting, building a good simple house is dull. Your chances of being happy with what you end up with are greatly enhanced if you stay away from the pros." Me: "You mean that? Architect: "Why give some asshole the chance to show off at your expense? Me, realizing that he wasn't referring to himself but rather to the class of architect whose fees I might be able to afford: "But, surely, the technical know-how . . . Architect: Nothing to it. All the pro does is keep a copy of Ramsey and Sleeper at hand. There's no need to actually *know* any of *that* shit . . .")

Know it? I can't even read it. To arrive at the most favorable total orientation they suggest algebraic formulas I just can't do. Pages and pages. I suppose some aren't as important as others. Do I need to know the amount of solar energy received on vertical surfaces ($R = {}^I D \times A \cos a$)? I'm relieved to read at the end of it all: "The expression 'total orientation' refers to both the physical and psychological side, the view and the privacy are aspects in orientation which *quite often* [my emphasis] override the physical considerations."

Then, alas, they continue: "Above all, as a building is only a mosaic unit in the pattern of a town organization, the spatial effects, the social intimacy, and its relation to the urban representative directions . . ." but I can't go on. Let's leave it that my research has done nothing to contradict my emotional preferences, as I suspected would be the case.

I constructed what I thought to be a reasonably accurate, unambiguous letter to Mr. L. "confirming our verbal agreement," asking that the house be set north-south by the compass. And since the magnetic variation around here is just under 13 degrees west of true north, that would give the west wall, where I wanted the windows, a slight, desirable southern tilt, the better to corral the winter sun.

I asked for a return acknowledgment, though I could see that Louie was not a man to put much store in letters and wasn't surprised when no answer came. But, Oh God, I wasn't prepared for the horror looming at us, leering at us the next Friday evening. A bunker, nay, the first ten stories of a highrise. What sins had I committed to have this visited on me? Louie must have brought in the forms and the cement trucks as soon as the dust had settled on our tracks. Ten, fifteen feet into the air, his forms looked as if they were meant for a section of the Maginot Line. I would have to build escalators to the front door. Disaster!

Almost. When I'd climbed up the forms I saw that the concrete hadn't been poured yet, only the footings, twice as wide as the twelve-inch foundation walls they would support. Of course, it was hard to tell where the eventual ground level would be, as there was a lot of fill to be brought in, to make the front of the house and the top of the hill meet. In the failing light I retrieved one of my strings and tied one end to a tree at ground zero and the other to the top of the form. A cliff was thus described! I realized darkly that something in my calculation had gone wrong. Downstairs, at the bottom of the dungeon, in the would-be cellar, there would be headroom enough for King Kong where I had thought to keep the ceilings as low as could be.

I wrote down a dream of that night: an enormous house, huge rooms going on and on, ceilings too high to be seen, towers, wine cellars, huge, hugely empty. Silent as a Queen's fart. And nobody home.

Early the next morning I drove down to the store to call Louie. He had already left. (Oh, God, why did I listen to that cynical architect. I needed someone to yell at.) But his good wife said that maybe I find him at construction site, Last Gasp Village, or at the garage. I said, Please, tell him don't pour. No trucks today. Okay? I surely sounded a lunatic, but perhaps she had read my letter? Find him easy, just ask for Louie. She wouldn't hear from him till suppertime. (Oh God!) But I went off to scare him up, thinking that the trucks would be coming in fleet strength as soon as I left. I would return, and the bunker would be there forever; in due course my little barn would sit on it pathetically, like Oliver Hardy's inadequate bowler.

Last Gasp Village was partially complete. "Entirely Electric Homes in a Planned Environment." How carefully put together, as if to apply the refinements of Suburbia to the Berkshire hills. There were builders about, all of them looking efficient and knowledgeable to my panicked eye, but no Louie. I decided that my place was at home, driving away the cement trucks. Speeding over the mountain I saw him: he actually did have another job close by.

He was putting up still more forms. I was worried? He come take a look, no sweat. No cement coming till next week 'cause footings gotta set. (Oh.) Yes, of course, I understand *that,* but what about those forms? Oh no, couldn't change forms now, cost too much. Everything like in letter.

I dreaded the idea of a drawn-out argument over who would pay for changes, though I thought my letter would give me an advantage. Surely he had made a mistake. When we went over the specs I would be firm but conciliatory. Alas, as soon as he started explaining it to me, I realized where I had made the mistake. My figuring had been done from the *low* point in the excavation. Of course he had to line everything up from the *high* point. Sokay, we just no pour in to top. How high you want? It would be eighteen inches lower, it was agreed.

See, he said, is simple job. But I wanted one more thing I just happened to think about: a four-inch setback at the eventual ground level so that I could face the wall with stone. Sokay, no charge because less cement don't cost so many. You sure that's all, now? (Vinegar? Mustard? Got enough eggs for breakfast?) He was after all a good provider. I believe he never read my letter. In any case I liked the fact that, after all my worrying about compass readings, the house is fixed on the line of that green string, which in turn was fixed to whatever was handy. No one but me and you will ever know.

It was now June, and my program was beginning to lag behind schedule. I needed to think about getting a floor

on that foundation (which first had to be backfilled),
establishing a better camp, getting aholt of some money.

The camp was the easiest part. We moved south along
the line of forest, where there was another shallow well
concealed by a new growth of spruce. There I cut a lot
of fir saplings and, using two large trees as the front
posts, made a sort of shed with them. This was covered
with heavy plastic and, behold, we had a "summer
kitchen." The site of a burned-down house in the field
below offered the shelves and warming oven from an old
stove, which seemed a fairly animal-proof way to store
food. (We had been plagued by skunks at the other site.
The skunks didn't go away, but they didn't get the food
either. At night you could hear them circling and circling, getting closer and closer to the fire. They were
often close enough to the firelight to seem part of the
company, and so they were.) The firebox from the same
stove served as a kind of oven during that summer; with
the fire in front of it potatoes cooked faster and more
evenly than under the coals.

This camp was also backed up against the woods and
even more susceptible to wet. The first rain—of many—
after the tent went up, I had to dig a trench around it to
drain off a pool of water.

Money was a more complicated problem. The $12,000
by this time was gone. The first payment to the Barnmover and the down payment on the land used that up;
to pay Louie I would take a "debt consolidation" install-
ment loan from the Friendly Bank in the city. The mortgage on the land cost $166.19 a month. My plan was to

get a building mortgage from the local bank, pay off Old Grimace gloating over his profits in the Heartland, have the remainder to build with; $26,000 worth of mortgage would give me a cool twelve thou for lumber, perhaps some paid help, plumbing. It seemed like enough. I went over the cost of all the lumber necessary for closing-in; for instance, I could get some locally cut, varied-width hemlock for board-and-batten siding at about twenty-one cents a foot. A lot of money, but a thousand feet is also a lot of boards. I needed about 3,000 feet, but as you always need more than you think, add at least 15 per cent —call it 3,500, or $735 worth. I was optimistic. The idea would be to tack up the green lumber using double-headed nails, take it all down after a year of drying and renail it for good. I didn't much like the idea, but it would be the cheapest. For roof-decking I would use matched 1×6 spruce at roughly the same price: cost about $650, plus shingles or maybe a metal roof.

Trouble was the first bank said flat out, after the necessary form-filling, that I couldn't possibly build the house for that kind of money. I thought, they are really saying that a house built so cheaply is beneath their dignity. I was mortified: my whole house was going to be built *for free,* using *recycled material!* . . . but there was a kind of deafness on the receiving end.

There was also another bank across the street. I got a haircut, imported a city jacket to wear with my jeans. The three of us went, cultivating a sense of promise, dedication, in another country the epitome of heroic socialist realism—three self-reliant figures leaning against an

inexplicable east wind, faces to the dawn. (The smallest
figure spoiled the image by being rather smelly. And he
drew some anxious glances as he reached for the V.P.'s
fascinating in-box.)

They wanted plans of some sort. How many square
feet? How many floors, bedrooms, toilets, showers?
What kind of heating? Attached or separate garage? I
couldn't say that no one would know until the time came,
that I didn't want to mess up my head with ideas con-
ceived in an anticipatory vacuum, that inspiration came
to me after I had hammer in hand.

Or perhaps I lacked the courage and the words to
make a case for amateurism in those neat, neo-colonial
surrounds. Would the Vice-President have understood if
I had said that I had no working plans, only ambitions?
That I wanted a house that would keep two or twenty in
reasonable comfort and some privacy, air-conditioned
the year round by the forest growing and overgrowing
just out there; a house that would open up in the spring
like a day lily and overlook November's wonderful sor-
rows with equal grace?

No, money requires a specific language and rightly so.
Sniffing the way the wind was blowing, I promised a floor
plan, and the man seemed pleased. He even suggested
that such a plan need not be exactly exact. Just something for the mortgage committee to have on file. Reasonable; and for my part I welcomed the idea that fiduci-
ary concerns would, for the moment, make it necessary
to forsake the burdensome vow of innocence.

During the next week I met with a young architect I

knew slightly. It wasn't as easy as all that, though. He had ideas of his own, some of them definitely seductive. How about four different levels, all a half-floor through more or less? Lots of balconies and windows at odds with each other? I liked it, but the thought of building all those staircases made me tired. How about decks? Too much the current mode. He showed me how easy it would be to lower one section of the main floor; he'd draw up the plans just the way I wanted, but wouldn't I allow him just this one aberration? So we ended up with two different sets of drawings, one his, one mine. I agreed that his plans would be more persuasive with the Mortgage Committee, but didn't he see that they would also involve me in a deception? I had applied for a building loan, that is, the bank pays out the mortgage money during the course of construction, reserving the right to inspect from time to time to make sure that construction is indeed coursing. If I didn't follow the plans submitted . . . I had a terrible vision of a delegation of Vice-Presidents appearing with steel measuring tapes, slide rules, a filing cabinet on self-propelled wheels (the head Veep would drive it like a golf cart).

I mailed the simpler set of plans. Thus were certain decisions made, or at least conflicting options eliminated, less for the sake of sound design and the accommodation of dreams, than for the principle of movement, of getting on with it finally. In fact those plans were never seen again. They served both bank and builder well nonetheless.

*   *   *

From the kitchen window you see the garden gate. Perhaps it is raining down in the valley; we are in a cloud that obliterates the rest of the world. Soon it will be fall again. Thanks to cyanide (I think) the garden is pouring forth a cornucopia of fresh vegetables.

The blueberries are an embarrasment of extraordinary riches, each one dripping with moisture now, fattening.

I remember worrying about that gate, having nothing to work with, no tools or lumber. It was a modest challenge, but the mocking voice that believed nothing would grow here, that the gardener was a wastrel and a false dreamer made it important. In the ruins I found three short lengths of oak from what looked to have been a chest of drawers. They became the sides and the diagonal of a gate that is otherwise maple sapling. Chicken wire was stretched over this frame. The hinges are bits of wire. And there is that burned-over drawer pull to give it class. I thought it would do for the first season, three gardens ago.

Those ruins also provided a usable pick head, an unusable axehead, the hearth stone—it had been used as a threshold, I believe. The retaining walls that eventually got built were quarried from the old stone foundation. But what I needed most had long since rotted: bits and pieces of wood in odd sizes, scrap, leftovers, anything milled. For instance we missed having a table at the camp. To prepare food, to put food down, to cut bread or slice a carrot requires a table, or something like it, with a smooth top. I thought of making one out of saplings, but is a corduroy-topped table a table at all? No wonder building a sawmill was first priority in these parts.

The detritus around the old barn was as high as the first story of the once-attendant farmhouse. The barn itself was laid out, most of it, on the ground, its parts grouped according to their function. There didn't look to be much of it in this unnatural state; just a lot of big timbers, some of them worse off than I had remembered. The Barnmover met me there. Yes, he would replace whatever timbers or parts thereof were rotted out. You couldn't tell till you was getting it back up what had to go where. 'Course most of them knee braces are all shot to hell, and now the bottom of them posts gotta go. But there's more good wood here than meets the eye. (What?) Well, yes, the rot had taken a couple of them pretty good, and anyways some had been cut off already years ago, when they put in a new foundation.

On general principles I thought the less you lose the better off you are. But he said, you get the ceiling too high, you don't see the beams. And in fact he was right. One post had to be replaced altogether: it had been under that leaky dormer. There was another that was just 9′10″ before real decay took over. So that's the height of the main room here. Ungainly, but I'm getting used to it. Originally from sill to wall-plate measured about 12′ 6″, I believe. If we'd bothered to splice the lengths needed on the bad posts, instead of chopping them off, there could have been a full second story. Now as then

HEADING FOR THE BARN

I would vote for keeping any barn at its original dimensions; but if surgery has to be done, then cut the damn thing down to a natural size; ceilings ten feet high in this climate? Are you crazy or what?

I was determined to find something useful in all that rubble, some souvenir of the "old barn" to live with. How innocent and urbane the eye that can look at such a pile of material and see almost nothing worth hauling away, only relics. If I looked at it now, after a couple of years of earnest recycling, the discovered wealth would convulse my New Englandized soul. For a hatchet carpenter like myself, there is nothing like a pile of planks of differing weights and lengths.

The bottom half of a plank door—perhaps the top of the table? some lengths of siding from a wall that hadn't been clapboard; nothing else seemed worth lifting out, de-nailing. In fact, culling through that hill of junk embarrassed me. People gawked at me from the road to Williamstown: sightseers, smart suburban matrons getting a little Mountain Air, families scouting expensive camps in Vermont. It isn't really the same as scavenging in city trash baskets, but do these people know that? Do they know that the scavenging rights to a burned-down house or barn would be *sold* at one time hereabouts.

Here comes the ex-barn-owner, walking slowly down the drive from his back stoop. I am a poacher and fear the worst. "Lotsa good stuff here," he says. "You gonna use them old boards?" I think: now he will put a price on them. "Be sure to take anything you want, now," he says, "ain't no good to me."

And then: "Found some cut nails about," he handed me a jelly glass full, "you might find a use for them, I guess."

The table is even now supporting the breakfast dishes, the barn-door top covered with a somewhat tattered oil-cloth, the maple legs and many braces firmly held together by these old cut nails. (I didn't know it at the time, but the fact is that when the green maple dries and shrinks it holds onta them cut nails like mean death. The table would last a lifetime, but all the diagonals among the legs make it impossible to sit at; I will have to remake it someday in the same mode.)

I had to start thinking about the wherewithal to hold up the first floor. I needed some big, heavy beams. The Barnmover had told me that I should frame the house in the conventional way, as he had done for himself. His idea was first to nail the inside, finished wall to the *outside* of the reconstructed barn frame, thus avoiding the difficulties of fitting around all those posts and braces. Then he framed 2×4's, still working from the outside, ran the usual wires and pipes, insulated, and tacked on the siding. It was clever but, I thought, unnatural, as it separated the barn frame from the house in a way that made the beams a cosmetic (plastic reproductions are the next logical step). Also working from the inside out supposes that time and money are available to do the whole job at once.

So without knowing the implications, I had already decided to keep the barn as barnlike as possible. I would stud up the walls *between* the posts, and I would frame the half floor downstairs with post and lintel, imitating the original as much as I was able. The Barnmover had some posts, but not 8 eight-footers. I would not, or could not, find them at the old site. I could get something cut at a lumberyard, or more likely have them cut to order.

I called a yard and was told they didn't do that sort of thing. I tried another and the boss wasn't there; the young guy on the phone thought I should knock together some 2×8's, or was I looking to go bankrupt? The boss didn't call back. I thought it a sign that I should start scavenging in earnest and without scruple.

On the first trip to see this land, the fall before, I had noticed an odd, square, three-story house in a state of great disrepair not more than three miles up the valley. All three floors had wraparound porches, or once did anyway, the underpinnings had given way on one side so that they had the appearance of a painting by Salvador Dali, one corner melting in the sun. The next time I looked the building—it had been a nursing home, I found out—was half demolished, and standing up through the debris were a number of heavy pillars, some of them still two or more stories proud.

I took to driving by. After several passes I made myself leave the car and move close enough to see that the posts were what I needed: hand-hewn 8×8's. But how come? Surely the building was turn-of-the-century, not before. Perhaps the beams had themselves been scavenged from an earlier structure, a huge barn maybe?

I coveted the nursing home. Piles of lumber, boards,

closets, moldings. It was great luck to find something so close, so rich. Collect everything, I would soon learn. No junk, but any piece of anything that looks usable, every solid piece of wood, every doorknob, and if you ask yourself the answer is always, "Take it."

Finally my covetousness overcame my shyness. I got my wife, who approved of recycling, to knock on the door of the neighboring house. A man down the street had the contract. I offered to work with him on the demolition; I would pay fifty cents a foot for any 8×8's I wanted. He wanted some stuff from the place, already had a stack of 3×4 studs he had taken out of the top floors; I could have my pick of the rest.

The place looked as if it would fall right over if you leaned against it seriously. We went around with the neighbor. There was still a staircase intact; indeed the first floor and part of the second seemed remarkably solid. The ground-floor porch was as good as the day it was made, with the exception of a few rotten floorboards and peeling paint. Inside, a turn-of-the-century interior: wallpaper over plaster, narrow beaded moldings, no insulation (the death of the place, I guess), rough-cut pine sheathing of varied widths, some boards two feet wide or more, knotty and split, grade "z" lumber. Four-pane windows of the period; the beams were the treasure.

The home had been built against a bank. The foundation in the back was some eight feet high or better. The retaining wall hit the building slightly forward of midships, convenient for throwing the debris down back, out of the way. It must have been forty-by-fifty feet, and in character someone old, angry at being made useless, by-passed, a spinster aunt no one wanted.

Tools? A crowbar, cat's-paw, sledge hammer? I confessed innocence of any such. I could see that the Designated Scavenger didn't like the sound of it. But I had a chainsaw! He lightened somewhat and allowed as how his sledge and a couple of crowbars would be at my disposal.

Early in the morning, the chrome on the relatively new station wagon blinks in the morning sun, wishing itself back in Westchester County. We approach the Home with hands visibly empty. (I'm not going to hurt you.) Christ. Where do you start? The front doorway loomed, lilacs blooming with bits of shingle and wood. The staircase didn't even talk back when kicked. The posts pointing up to the nonexistent third floor were still festooned with a broken lacework of plaster, lathing, faded pink flowers fluttering in the morning air. The blueness of the sky gave the certain promise of a hot, merciless day.

We were the first there, glad to have something to do together, the baby would be entertained by one of his half-sisters. I supposed you first took out the windows, doors. We started at a side window downstairs, out of sight. Carefully, so as not to ruin trim, pulling it off with the claw side of the hammer. Then the clapboards. But that required taking off the trim of the other windows, that is, if the siding was going to come off in one piece —and a door to the porch, too. A kind of jackstraws. Perhaps it should be done inside out. I thought of all the demolitions I had stopped to watch on New York City streets. Didn't the guts always come out first?

Help arrived. He suggested we get after the posts upstairs. So, first the remains of the walls. Mouse turds, old shredded newspapers; here's the sledge: bang, smash and over the side. Violence was the active ingredient here, not salvation. We thought it was not a place for women and children; too many jagged ends, rusty nails, splintering pine boards that cared not for the sanctity of human flesh. But there was a stream running through a meadow high with grass just in the back. My support wandered off.

We cut the posts so that they fell heavily on the porch, which didn't budge. I became more familiar with the crowbar and sledge hammer as the day progressed. You don't start with the windows; you have no time for jackstraws. The pace quickens; the vengeful spirit calls out for greater and greater satisfaction. When that bit of flooring doesn't want to come out, I think, men nailed it together, and this man can take it apart. The sweat pours down, showering from my face as the sledge hits the joist. There, it moved. Take the leather work-gloves off, get a better swing. Two more blows, three at most. And what a visceral, happy screech as the nails pull out and a whole section responds to gravitational force, gathers speed, falls away—instant empty space. The next catastrophe will be bigger still. Recycling is an abstract idea; destruction is fun.

I had thought that with luck we could have the place down in the course of the weekend. I worked Sunday alone, however; the D.S. had other things on his mind. Most of the following weekend too. But I was getting good. I bought a new chain for the saw, the first having been worn to the nub on old nails. I used it with *awful* abandon.

The ground-floor porch had to go. I tried in my mind taking it apart post by post, railing by railing. It wouldn't play on the streets of New York, where the professionals practice their trade. I smashed in all the floorboards around the walls upstairs, exposing from the top the joists that attached the roof of the porch to the side of the house. On the ground floor again, I cut all the posts save one just above floor level, with the chainsaw; then the joists on top. Physics told me that the things would slide outward. I cut the last joists mighty carefully. Nothing. I pushed with me feet; yes, I think so. The siding was holding it still. A couple of whacks with the sledge. Push again, sitting on the upstairs sill, the legs pushing out, out. Slowly and then with a rush the whole thing fell out and collapsed, bounding and breaking on the retaining wall, raising a cloud of dust. Alas, there were no sidewalk attendants, no applause.

It felt good anyhow. A long, dirty day's work with a bath in the cold stream as pay. But it wasn't the job that would keep the union together. The wrecking ball is a male tool, after all. Perhaps when it came to hammer and nails our rhythms would more nearly match.

Unluckily in the city I saw an ad for a '63 Ford pickup, good running order, needs body work. Obviously what my image needed. Starting in the early morning, through a misty, sleepy country, rattling northward. No radio, a sense of isolation, windows open to vent the carbon monoxide. It seemed to be rather unsafe at speed (i.e. down hill) and to have some difficulty with the inclines. Still, we made it in good time for lunch, both of us singing up the gravel road.

There to greet us was the foundation, gleaming and new, shorn of its forms: a cygnet, a promise rather than a thing of beauty. It still looked like a bunker. But the windows were in the right place, and by God there was a lot of cement standing on that rock.

Running about, like my dog first in the country after a long winter wading through the gutters of New York, round and round. Climbing to the top. It's just a foot wide, but I can stand here at the corner and look down the valley. This is the kitchen, the door here facing south, and the grass is green to the edge of the stone retaining wall. The wall will extend from the house in a great arch to join the other where a barn once was, and in decades hence someone will not know what to make of the differences and samenesses.

I climbed down to get a frontal view of it. *Someone has made a mistake!* That southerly, expensive basement window, one of only two for the bathroom downstairs, is right under where the door would have to be: any stairs or stoop would cut off all the light it could manage to gather. Shit. I could move the imaginary door? Change the kitchen? But I will worry about it tomorrow; there'll be nothing to build with at all until the beams get here.

HEADING FOR THE BARN

Parked in front of the leveled Home, the truck seemed to have found just the right environment for its Golden Years. Did it feel up to doing a little work? On investigation it was found that the usefulness of its underpinnings was in doubt. The man at the garage took one look and shook his head. How much you pay for that [worthless piece of junk] he wanted to know. I believed with some coaxing, together we could make a comeback, but, alas, not the big leagues right away.

The Designated Scavenger, who had not been all that much in evidence my last couple of days at the Home, decided I needed him now. He was right. He was one of those fortunate people who have faith in machines. I would have used block and tackle to get those things out of where they lay, like so many dead soldiers, in and around the wreckage. He had a long piece of chain. One end hooked to the frame of his station wagon, and the other to a beam. I cleared the way of major obstructions, and he gunned it down the Home's generous parking lot, my posts smoking angrily after him.

Lined up, the treasure was dirty and strong. The uprights had been pine; the upstairs sills, oak. Heavy as steel, they seemed, all pegged together in the manner of a barn, perhaps the work of some frustrated barn-builder? Certainly the tight mortise-and-tenon joining was the best way, but it seemed extraordinarily labor-intensive in the era of cheap nails. Or was it meant for me all along? I had almost 142 feet of 8×8's and another 50 feet of smaller beams. It had cost only $71; not counting $150 for the truck, hands so full of splinters they creaked in the night, a kneecap swollen from a misstep through a rotten floorboard. I asked for help manhandling them into my new toy; they would go one at a time up the hill. The longer ones would have to be cut, I guessed. Predictably this wasn't good enough for a machine-oriented fellow. You oughtta rent a real truck, he said.

Then Mr. Louie came by to ask if everything was in accord with my fantasies; fast enough? On the schedule just like he said, no? I could have used a level, tested for plumb, considered the implications of an entirely too-permanent puddle that stood inside the footings, just under the bathroom. But it all looked fine to me, and I handed over the last of the money from the bank loan. I also asked him where I could rent a truck for a couple of hours. Use one of mine. Where you need? Five bucks? He even delivered it to the parking lot.

So how do you get the beams up onto the bed of a six-wheeled dump truck? Knock together a ramp from lengths of scrap, run the chain over the cab, gun the wagon and up they go. Neat. The chain is heavy and gets heavier every time I have to take it back to hook up another one. But the machine is doing the real work. The truck's loaded in no time and then (of course) won't start. It's a diesel, and we don't know how. On the phone Mr. Louie says leave it there, loaded, he'll pick the truck up and dump the goods at my front door all in the same motion. No, no, no money, is all right, glad to help.

As the Home stopped resisting the wrecker's improvements, its integral parts assumed a valuable, separate identity; perhaps my eye could not see the detail as long as the whole retained some integrity. There was one corner of the site for lengths of the beaded molding, another for usable studs and planking, a third for "specials": the plank door to the cellar—for some reason faded into a subtle shade of purple, a narrow closet door that came out sash and all, some 3 × 10 pine boards that might do for a counter. Load after load, the little truck took them up the hill, valiantly, patiently, first gear most of the way.

Almost every scrap that was thus removed has been used. (I wonder, where is the rest of that molding?) There comes a time when the labor required to pull out old nails, to design the building to accommodate erratic materials, is a prohibitive cost. Still, every sagging barn or burned-out, abandoned house I see becomes material for another structure, a game like anagrams; more fun even than lumberyards, and psychologically uplifting in the bargain.

Great pile of beams and scavenge sitting in front of the new foundation. I had to think hard to remember what that patch of overgrowth had looked like just a month or so before. The cement was strangely pleasing, strong, clean, simple. I liked its temperature and its texture. The outside needed to be covered with tar, to seal it prior to trucking in the backfill (another $360 I hadn't counted on). Terrible sloppy job: the tar gets on everything (plan to throw away the clothes you wear), but you don't get to do the job over again, so do it right. The Barnmover has cautioned me: lay an underground drain at the base, where the footings meet the rock, to carry the water around the house. But the wrong kind of pipe comes back from the long trip to the building supply place (I should have bought it myself when I thought of it weeks ago, damn it!) So, forget it, it's Sunday night, the backfill is coming on Wednesday; we're going to be away for two weeks. And there's two feet of cement there; the way the rock slopes, the water should be running parallel to the wall anyway. (That's one Sunday afternoon I'd like to live over again!)

Perhaps I'm not thinking right; the brain is muddled; another of the basement windows is out of place: directly under a major post, a structural disaster. If I had drawn an elevation of the front it would have been obvious right away. So a piece of steel bracing will have to go over that window, on top of the foundation. (But what will that do to the sill?)

A week later we fetched up for several days at an island farm in British Columbia. Old missionary farmhouse, a stand of virgin timber, Douglas fir and cedar, rolling fields edged with the calm waters of a bay. Sheep pasture, goat's milk (and cheese—I'd like myself better if I could stomach it). I worked one day putting in fencing. Efficient work with a tractor-driven posthole digger enhanced by occasional glimpses of snow-covered mountains in the distance. At the end of the day the boss says: "Five dollars a day and all you can eat. How about it?"

A tempting offer. Let someone else worry about the

mortgage, the electricity line, the approaching winter storms. I thought, I could be happy doing this for a long time. Clear the head of all this nonsense about ownership, capital improvement. The hired man surely is better situated in the present; anyway, inflated land values are injurious of the commonweal, as Henry George pointed out, and not to be played with.

And yet, and yet. . . . The flesh is weak and needs posterity, needs an accumulation of goods, a visible trail, riches earned and otherwise. (Could it be that the sense of homesteading as a sound *business* venture is the salt in an otherwise nutritious but bland loaf?) The process once begun could not be truncated, and I came back feeling only slightly disloyal.

Cool summer morning; mist in the trees, everything wet from the night's heavy dew. Shafts of sunlight pouring through the branches; another miracle of dawning, the maples in proudest leaf, waiting for their daily blessing as the sun climbs.

I had started out from the city on dark streets, dead save for the rumble of trucks like tanks on the avenues. Even the endless public life of Harlem was flickering out as I drove through—occasional lighted doorways, a returning reveler, insomniacs, addicts, children without beds, at least beds of their own. In the projects, always that light that wasn't turned off—a child afraid of the dark or people making love as a honky's car with Massachusetts plates makes for the bridge. Most of the journey is through an alien country filled with strange people whose good will one is wise not to take for granted, a gulf separating the countries of my dual citizenship.

But as I crossed the border into Massachusetts, as night gave over to an August day, there was for the first time that sense of a returning rather than an excursion, a sense of heading for the barn. Would the man who had so blithely said he would truck in some gravel have actually done that, with no one at home to tell him how or where? Would the temporary walls at the end of the foundation not have collapsed under the weight of the (no doubt) carelessly dumped backfill? (The "walls" had gone up quickly before we left: logs culled from the first site-clearing and stacked between uprights dug into the ground, the whole given a mean inward slant and braced with stout birch and maple saplings. It was not believed by others that it would hold.) Would my piles of invaluable, valueless junk not have been spirited away or sunk back into the ground in the meantime?

The leafy-ness is startling. It is quiet and new on the hilltop. The gravel all seems to be there, making for the first time a meeting between field and foundation, like gums growing around a new tooth. The temporary retaining walls have held their own. It looks like a place waiting to be built, an amphitheater dressed and ready for players.

VI

Marginal Differentiation and the Idea of Progress

A market town, Western Massachusetts, seven A.M. Waiting for the stores to open. Men at the counter of Mary's Restaurant, backs bowed over their coffee cups: perhaps the woman in the white nylon uniform is Mary. First names: Is Janie feeling any better? . . . Wassat Bette's cousin Jack I saw down the street yestiddy? . . . I am a stranger. I hunch my back over my coffee cup, smile at the woman who might be Mary.

There are two hardware stores in town. One still has a wall of floor-to-ceiling cabinets and drawers, worn, squeaky wood underfoot. It also has a smaller inventory, must be more expensive, and is seldom crowded. The store is to me what a good delicatessen is to a gourmand. Everywhere I look there is something I can't live without. I need so much in the way of tools that it undermines my confidence. (What am I doing here? What do I know about building a house?) A pick handle, rope, pulleys, nails, two large "unbreakable" chisels. The electric tools are Christmas in another land.

Then, with reluctance, to the lumberyard. I need uniformity, and here's the right place to look: 2×8's to cap the foundation, to have something to drive a nail into. And one steel brace for that window. I make it known that I am starting a house over yonder. Will they deliver? Of course. There is a cash-and-carry yard in the next town; how much does civility cost in the wood business, I wonder. The way lumber is sold, by board-foot, square-foot, by size—$2'' \times 4''$ is actually $1\ 1/2'' \times 3\ 1/2''$ now, a $1'' \times 8''$ can be $11/16'' \times 7\ 5/16''$ or otherwise, depending—seems calculatedly obfuscating. Pocket computers have speeded up the billing process but done nothing to make it more intelligible. Still, people who work in lumber tend to be pleasant, friendly sorts. Later I would learn that there is often a price difference from yard to yard, and an even greater difference in the quality of the lumber, depending on the vagaries of the mills, the drying process. It pays to look around if time allows.

This was an important day. Work—carpentry—was actually starting. I was expecting a friend of a friend (would he actually show up?) who had said he would spend a few weeks working with me. Asking around for help had been a concession to practicality I had not wanted to make. I had thought that, given time enough and the will, I could manage the whole thing myself. The Home had given me other and more educated thoughts. I began to think in engineering terms: constructing some kind of derrick to lift those huge beams, setting them on the posts. And first I would have to drag them into place—with rollers? block and tackle? There was no way to put a car to work; a jeep with a winch would have been the thing, had one been handy somewhere. I still maintain it could have been done, but not if there was to be a shelter here when the wind blew the leaves from the trees and all life looked to winter quarters. (Every year the long, blue, promising days of August flash by in a greater blur. My very skin could sense the shortening days.) Egomaniacal self-sufficiency would have to go underground for the time being.

Skip was there when I returned, wondering where I had taken myself. He was smaller than I remembered, wiry and anxious to get to work, setting a businesslike, splattered, painter's cap over his long hair, amused at the idea that there were no plans on paper. He had been doing small contracting in the suburbs, where specifications and showing them are an important part of the game.

So let's get going. The trunk of Skip's car reveals a professional-looking set of tools, extension cords, bar clamps—the lot. He'd fitted a hammer holster to his belt; that was something I had to get. It advertised hard work, efficiency, sound proletarian aspirations. That clothing manufacturers recognize this now, put useless hammer-loops and rule-pockets in checked polyester bell bottoms, proves the point.

I thought our first task would be to chisel out the sill to accommodate the iron brace over the putative window. Skip pointed out, gently, that we could make up the quarter of an inch when we notched the joists. Yes, but would we remember?

Did we need a secretary? We would remember because we were gonna do it right. *Right?*

Drill holes in the 2×8's to fit the bolts imbedded in Mr. Louie's good cement. Skip stops to sharpen the hand drill when I would have just leaned on it a little harder. The job's done in an hour. (I have spent longer than that *thinking* about it.) What's next? Posts for the ground-floor back. Chainsaw is fueled and ready to go. Skip says: "Did you know the foundation is cracked?"

What? Say that again. From the trunk of his car he removes a level. The side wall is indeed cracked and leaning perceivably. Skip thinks the truck may have gotten too close to it when the backfill came in. The crack seems to be superficial. It had better be 'cause there ain't much to do about it now. However it means that we shouldn't rely on the foundation for the accuracy of our floor measurements. I was slow to grasp this sort of thinking: the interdependence of all parts of the structure, that a piece of carpentry is only as good as its most vulnerable join.

Impatience. T'hell with it. We measured out the posts, choosing which and what to cut to avoid useless leftovers.

But how do you cut these things square? In the first instance they did it by hand saw, but they must have had some kind of jig. We marked the 8×8's with a floor square on all four sides. But the damn thing itself isn't square. Lay it on a sawed 3×8 from the Home, mark it with the square at right angles to the board. Both sides and across the top. That supposes a relatively straight 8×8. Anyway, check for old nails, let fly.

Very satisfactory cut, but not quite straight. I'm pressing the saw. Don't. Let the tool do the work. The next one is better, but it takes both of us. One to work the chain, the other to watch the blind side, to make sure the blade doesn't crawl out of line. Even so they're not exactly square-cut, and one's so bad it has to be put aside for some other use.

These posts we can wrestle down inside the foundation and footings, only being careful not to drop them on our toes. Before that job's done Skip raises his fist in the air and brings it down twice, making at the same time a noise by which I'm supposed to believe the lunch whistle has blown. It is time: just noon, and we are working union hours.

But what union hall is as nice as ours, down the hill, in the cool of the young spruce. We could stop by the unruly garden on our way, thinning carrots, picking radish, lettuce, parsley, chives; tomatoes are on their way. There's cheese in the bucket floating in the well, and some cold beer gleaming from its dark bottom, attached to a string. As our lunches have not been prepared for us it's allowed that lunch continue until twelve forty-five, almost one by the time we're back on the line.

Each 8×8 post will be joined to an 8×8 joist in a series of post-and-lintel constructions along the ground-floor rear. The joists will be notched to receive the square-

ended posts. No barn-builder would have been satisfied
with such a shoddy joining, but would have made a tenon
in each post, probably notched the joists, as well as cutting a mortise to fit the tenon. We figure that the spikes
we toe-nail in will make up the difference. They don't, of
course. It's a serviceable piece of carpentry with the
floorboards holding it firmly together, but it has not the
elegance, strength, durability of the original.

And in another concession to time and the skills available, I have opted to use sawn lumber for the long first-
floor sill at the back. These 2×8's can be set into notches
on the outside face of the posts, making unnecessary the
more complicated and conventional three-way connection (sill, post, joist). It was a mistake from the point of
view of the interior: inside, the room lacks a cornice,
which by rights should be there. Structurally I think we
got away with it, but only by using heavy timbers as
added floor sills upstairs, so that the weight of the barn
frame is better distributed.

But those were details still to be worked out as we went
along, lining up the posts along the backside of the foundation, one under each of the timbers that would divide
the bays of the barn.

Only, wait a minute! (This was the sort of thing that
kept me up at night.) The siding wouldn't reach all the
way from peak to ground; there would be, should be a
break somewhere. If so, the siding for the lower part
should slide under the upper boards, meaning that the
posts I was putting up should recede from the edge of
the foundation about an inch, or the depth of the siding.

On the other hand (stay with this just a little longer, it will be over soon and won't be repeated) that got us in other trouble. The idea I had picked up was to be sure that everything drained directly into the ground, and it wouldn't if rainwater from the walls had a chance to drip onto the top of the foundation.

I argued that it was easy to gain or lose an inch here or there, that we should go on. My colleague argued that we should get it right the first time, not court later troubles, meaning that we had to figure out *now* how the upper part would be sheathed, and with what. My view was molded by a past full of error. Even if I thought I had it right now, there was a good chance time would prove me wrong, so why worry about it? Solutions would certainly appear (albeit difficult ones) at the right time. Thus does ignorance fortify itself, allowing the amateur to continue on his eccentric way unimproved and happy.

This discussion closed our first working day. A difference of ideology underlay it. We agreed to disagree, and as to the practical question, well, it was my place, wasn't it? Against Skip's experience and professionalism, I pitted my instincts to keep it simple, do one thing at a time, let it grow. Indeed there could be no other way for me; the idea that incontrovertible plans should be made in the abstract was infinitely frightening.

The northwest corner went up first. I stood the post on the sill and held it there while Skip braced it in place with a length of scrap lumber. We had found that the cement at the corner had been broken off by a piece of equipment; a rock was wedged underneath the post. We laughed and I thought of disaster. If we had some cement . . . ? But we didn't. (Would it all be like this, endless makeshifts?)

The first outside joist, a sill looked at from the point of view of the main floor, had the northern foundation wall as half its support. Twenty-seven feet long, it had probably been a tiebeam at the Home. We bullied it to its final resting place, lifting first one end then the other; finally Skip slid it out along the concrete on rollers made of logs while I held up the end with the help of another piece of log, walking it out the last couple of feet (always ready to scamper if I felt it getting out of control), toward that forlorn post waiting there eager to be part of something. There you are, another couple of inches, settling it down easy on its notch. Well, well, *well,* looky there, post and lintel, a pleasure to look at, walk under; basic, perfect, as fine and triumphant as any Roman construction and a good deal more satisfactory.

Well, that's fine for the outside, but now we have to lift the heavier oak joists straight up from the ground. I have foreseen the difficulty, hence the rope and pulley. Our sky hook is a tripod of three small ash trees no more than three or four inches in diameter but long and uniform from lifetimes spent looking for sunlight. These we lashed together with a length of clothesline I had been saving for just this moment, clinched the line down with nails, hung the pulleys from it and raised it hand over hand. It was heavy and awkward, a good sixteen feet high. We had to walk it around to get the thing into place. Then we lashed the single pulley to the beam going up. Heave gently; what a miracle is the mechanical advantage, how pleasant the watery sound of line running through blocks. The beam can be raised easily with two of us hauling, but it's unstable; it dips, slips a little in its noose, suddenly one end is on the ground.

We both had agreed that it would not be a good idea to try to lean the beam against the post: it's too heavy, the post too easily dislodged. Looking at the beam tilted up there makes it seem easy. I hold on while Skip braces a good-sized tree trunk against the post. Slowly I let it down, rest one end on top of the post. Okay! Now slip the lashing down the beam to raise the other side. Haul away. But of course the pressure is all outwards, and the beam immediately noses the post out of the way. I see it teetering ("Get out of the way!") and there is nothing to do but let them both fall, smack, into the mud.

On the second try we got the beam suspended, level, and needed only to bring it down so that both ends arrived on top of the respective posts at more or less the same time. But that meant that one of us had to take the rope (me) and also get up on a step (a cutoff beam end), act as guide with one hand, winch with the other. It couldn't be done. We needed another sort of rig or, preferably, another pair of hands.

At that moment, as by a signal, my sister arrived, quite proud of herself for having found us. Here, sister, hold this a moment! Just hang on. Thank you so much for coming. Aren't you glad you're here! How are you? Now let it down—careful! A moment of sweat and groans (it didn't do her hands any good), and that was that. We climbed on top, finding it almost impossible to get a nail into the oak. We should drill holes for these nails. But with a hand drill? Let me have a go with that small sledge, sir.

The day was hot. We had spent the better part of it doing things badly. One more before the day is over? Getting the posts up was easy, especially as we had another hand to hold the thing in place while we both spiked it into the sill. The joist, another block of steel-like oak, slid into position on the ground (there's still mud on it if you look carefully). We were tired and could not fight it. Tie the block on it, pull, up she goes, easy. This time we have taken pains to see that the beam is balanced on the rope, that the tripod is exactly above and in line with the two posts. Up it went, with just one of us guiding it. Swing it over and around slightly, let it come down. We didn't get it on the first try, but on the second. Amazing! It all depends on where you put your tripod, as anyone could tell you. It took us only a day to learn. It's not that we're stupid, you see, it's simply that we wanted it to be hard, heroic; we needed to be worn down to see the problem clearly. Now we were pros and the job finished!

In place, the frame looked like an overgrown grape trellis, each grape would be as big as an orange. Or a Cretan ruin, but the posts would be stone columns, arms reaching out of the ground, a grillwork against the summer sky.

I ask why we didn't assemble each unit on the ground, lift them up with pikes and ropes, as barns were always made. That simplest of ideas surely had occurred to me; I must have discarded it for some reason. Or was it that it would have been too easy? Unchallenging?

Skip was tape-crazy. Measuring every which way all the time. Parallels, diagonals, pressing the level against the posts, straightening, rebracing, moving things by fractions of an inch. (I remember a Saturday morning at the lumberyard, a thin old carpenter who seems to be there out of habit, or hope. He takes a folding rule out of the pocket in the leg of his overalls, unfolding, refolding, sliding it back with a little lift of the knee; then the gestures are repeated, as someone else would adjust his spectacles or chew gum.) So much of carpentry is getting the distances right.

But I didn't know that yet. One hut is much like another, and the frightening prospect of construction to last a lifetime hadn't penetrated my impatience. Another function of impatience is faulty sequencing. We spent the next couple of days cutting a broad mortise in those major joists to fit in the lesser beams that would tie the whole together, a job ten times more difficult now that the beams were suspended eight feet in the air.

This needs explanation: I had decided to use a heavy decking to do away with the usual joists (i.e. 2×8's on sixteen-inch centers). After this grillwork of beams had been assembled, a floor of three-inch laminated spruce would go directly on it. The Barnmover thought this an unsound plan. He liked the conventional way and wondered what I would do to hide the plumbing and wiring. He suggested that you can always fit the beams in, afterwards even, but that I would never regret having a real sturdy floor.

I figured I could make a sturdy floor my own way, and if we did the job right the three-inch flooring would also be the *finished* floor. I would save myself the cost (and labor—a considerable savings, since we would be sawing everything by hand for the time being) of laying in joists, covering them with plywood, then having to find the money for some pine or hardwood flooring. The only drawback might be that such a floor would be noisier, although that would affect just the one room downstairs. On the other hand it would be cheaper, faster, and most importantly would maintain the structural integrity of the barn. There were calls all over New England to locate the flooring (the telephone company never loses). In the end I found some at a yard outside of Boston, after calling the firm that mills the stuff in Seattle. All this had been accomplished just the week before. I had sent them a certified check for $1,512.19 of additionally borrowed money. On Saturday they would send me out a truck with 3,640 board feet of 3×6 laminated (three-ply) yellow pine decking.

Paying back that money was another problem; the mortgage wouldn't be coming through for a couple of weeks at least, presuming there would be no embarrassing questions at the bank. In the meantime the sun shone out of a clear August sky. We had discovered the blueberries and had been forceably reintroduced to silence, to hand tools, to a natural and cooperative working rhythm.

The timbers we were working had been rafters once: spruce, with a satisfactory taper to them. My hammer rested on my hip in a holster made of leather with a steel loop; the handle banged against my thigh, friendly and comforting. Reaching for it I would wait for my body to assume a half-crouch, the sound track from *High Noon* drumming in my ears, a gunman at my back. But all I had to hit was the shank of the chisel. Making tenons: saw across the grain, split with the grain. Pay attention. It is soon easy to gauge how much needs to be cut with the saw—rather too little than too much—when the chisel will bite cleanly, when to curse the knots. Paying attention requires actually seeing the wood curl off the cutting edge, watching the event itself, like seeing the ball hit the bat.

Taking chunks out of the 8×8's was a different matter. (Not to have done this while they were still on the ground was plain lunacy.) Digging out a mortise you always have to cut across the grain; the chisel is inefficient though necessary. The old-timers would first drill out the corners of the mortise from the top, then saw through the beams as much as possible, dig out the rest with the chisel. We could see the mark of their tools in the mortise already made (we would re-use them whenever we could). By the time these beams had been worked a brace and bit had been invented that fit over the beams and could be driven with a bicycle-like foot pedal, though more commonly it would be fitted to a shoulder brace. However no one solved the problem presented by having to cut out a pocket across the grain. The chainsaw is the answer, of course, provided you keep it steady, don't hit any hidden nails, and are careful not to press the chain hard against the back of the notch. (It will buck, threatening to fly up into your pretty face.) Brilliant idea, teeth on a chain. Why not the same on a shoulder brace, hand-turned, using a gear reduction? Of course, it would have to be a smaller chain with a much narrower kerf. The technology was available by the 1870's—we made machine guns, after all. I suppose a professional would not see the need for such a newfangled time-saving invention.

We spent all that day and most of the next building mortise and tenon, the sun beating down. I straddled the newly installed timber, cutting away with a chisel, eight feet in the air, watching the old dry oak come away in unforgiving splinters, a golden, almost orange color underneath. It split true along the grain, delightfully. It didn't at all like being dug at. Approach it squarely, firm but not frantic blows with the hammer against the chisel. This wood is living by a different clock: a hundred years old and just beginning its useful life. It is necessary again to remember to slow down. To pay attention, watch for the streaks of black which give away the site of invasion by a bit of steel. Watch the cutting edge: I am beginning to get the hang of this chisel. How much time had I spent with one before seeing/feeling the difference between cutting with the flat side and cutting with the beveled side? The angle is all-important; the cutting edge is delicate, no match for one of those old nails: one slip and there's a hideous nick, as if the revenging nail had taken a bite out of the encroaching blade.

There's another done. The newly cut wood is sensual, pleasant to the touch. Standing up requires some care, feeling the tenseness in the back and the slight dizziness, a brush with the possibility of falling. But I find eight inches wide enough to walk along without distress. Jumping down from the front end of the foundation there's a tingle in my feet as the veins and arteries get back to work.

Something directs my eyes overhead, to a blue nothing in back of the overhanging maples, green and blue and the sensation of everything growing, tentacles in the earth and air. A breath briefly rearranges the leaves overhead and fades into the sounds of whispering field-grass and bees in the milkweed. A moment of unexpected heavy silence, the frame freezes. I am drowning in chloroplasts, can't feel where my feet end and the soil begins, a moment of perfect balance.

It occurred to me then that there was nowhere else I'd like to be in the world, nothing else I'd like to be doing.

And then in the vacuum left by the moment's passing, a host of narrow-minded worries sprang up: would this floor be rigid enough, would the yard send out the truck on time, why hadn't I heard from the bank, the electric company, had I sent a check to Old Grimace? My wife and youngest child were on the other side of the continent wondering whether another crossing over was worth the effort. My children should be here, feeling their sneakers dissolve into the earth.

We were picking out the last of the minor joists, looking them over critically, the emphasis (unfortunately for the floor) on aesthetics (Question: can a timber that is inadequate to the job still be a thing of beauty; did we fail in both realms?), waiting for the lunch whistle to blow. Skip heard a truck rattling along the road. It was coming from the wrong direction but sounded like a truck that was looking for a building site. Sure enough, as it passed we could see through the trees that it was the expected vehicle piled high with lumber come all the way from Beantown.

It had rattled by at a good clip, but Skip ran after it anyway. "Hey, lumber, lumber. HEY, LUMBER!" He was like a man with a terrible thirst running after a water carrier on the edge of the Sahara. The truck kept to its erroneous way, on down to the village. We were waiting by the side of the road when it reappeared.

The driver, a loner, was not pleased with his day thus far. "Jesus fuckin' Christ," he said, leaning out of the cab, shifting gears. "They didn't tell me you was way the fuck out in the Mother-fuckin' boondocks." He looked down at us with considerable scorn. "How the fuck kin I get this shit where it's goin'?"

He had to go to the top of the hill, where there is a break in the trees, come down through the field in the track made by the cement trucks, then out through the old driveway. The green, scarred stake truck, top heavy with my floor, came at us through the grass like a Panzer Mark IV, but backwards. We watched from the corner where he had to turn sharply if he was going to make it to the foundation. Skip signaled him to slow down. The answer was a short blast of the horn which translated: "Move your ass outa there."

MARGINAL DIFFERENTIATION AND THE IDEA OF PROGRESS

But he didn't make the turn. The soil had been chewed up by the cement trucks; the new assault was too much for it. The back started around all right, but the cab just kept sliding almost gracefully downhill, like an old dancer, coming to rest with the nose of the truck almost up against a maple tree. There was no going forward. In reverse the wheels spun, tipping the load dangerously to leeward.

The trucker stepped down, tall, a hunter's cap, and bad teeth in a lean, lined face. A heart tattooed on his left arm said "Grace."

"Fuckin' hell." He kicked at the back wheels. "Fuckin' fuckers didn't tell me you was out in the fuckin' boondocks or I fuckin' well wouldna drove this fucker." He kicked at it again, missing, I remember. "Fuckin' dolly wheels aren't no fuckin' good." He looked at us as if for sympathy. "Fuckin' fuckers never tell ya fuckin' *nothing. Son-of-a-BITCH.*" This last, clearly enunciated in case his meaning might be mistaken, was delivered to the fantastic vault of blue enclosing our hilltop.

We got to work with the shovel, putting dry dirt underneath the wheels. No good. "Fuckin' sonabitch dolly wheels." (Meaning that power was transferred to only one set of the double rear wheels, we guessed.) Unloading here meant that each length of flooring would have to be carried the last thirty yards. But there was nothing else to do. Piece by piece Foulmouth slid them out to us to stack according to length. By the end of the hour the stacks were five feet high, two planks wide, an alleyway, a maze. The thought that we had to handle them all again was incapacitating.

Foulmouth had not turned off his engine nor separated himself from his inadequate equipment for more than the time it took to urinate on the obstructing maple. He was tying things down as if he were going somewhere when I suggested he share our simple, and much delayed, midday meal. We'd cope with his predicament after. He looked interested but surprised; instead of answering he said, "You fuckers got a shit load of work to do, looks like." Then, locking in the tailgate, "Shoulda gotten this fuckin' lumber upta the fuckin' house." At least that's what I thought I heard him say, though perhaps it was just a projection of my Utopian-Socialist inner ear.

We left him trying to get out of this effing backwater by himself; we listened to the profane roar of the diesel as we sat in our cosy lunch room, sorting out the splinters. We had lost a couple of hours as a result of our impetuous friend's stupidity; getting to a phone, calling a wrecker would be an added drag. The indefatigable engine spoke again. Fuckin' dolly wheels . . . Mothering boonies . . . Was there anything ever so inexpressibly funny? Fuckin' (groan gasp) dolly wheels . . . Dolly wheels! . . . Tears of laughter washed over the landscape, cascaded onto my bread and cheese, mixing with the mayonnaise. We hafta help the poor bastard out after all. Give him a beer and a ride to town.

But now there is an inexplicable silence from his quadrant. Walking up, we find that he has flown, vamoosed, disappeared, assisted no doubt by the strength of his incantations, without which he would surely still be ma rooned. There's no saying how he managed to extricate himself.

We would have been ready to tack some of that floor down the next day except for the need—God help us— to do some planning. Provisions had to be made for a stairwell somewhere. And if that had to be worked out, then I also had to figure out where the fireplace was going to be. How big is a stairwell? Indeed how big are stairs? Ramsey and Sleeper know. Three feet wide for residences, they say, although it can be less. We try to map the stairs themselves with less success. The Uniform Building Code says that you're not supposed to build stairs with a riser more than eight inches high, and the American Insurance Association says that the tread oughtn't to be more than nine inches wide, all of which does away with the narrow, angled stairways I like so well, winding around in back of the chimney. (The rule-of-thumb is: tread plus riser equals 17 inches, approximately.)

Since I wasn't sure where the floor would be downstairs, calculating exactly how many stairs were necessary, given an eight-inch riser, was frustrating. A good guess? What if it came to ladders? Surely some clever device could be worked out to get a human body up (or down) those eight feet (approximately), though stairs are fairly clever to begin with. On my floor plan a conventional, straight-run staircase would take out more living space than could be spared, I thought. So we decided to plan for twelve 8″ risers with a landing in the middle;

counting a nine-inch tread that was 54 inches laterally: but, hold it, the landing had to allow convenient turning room. The book says that the average human is assumed to be 22 inches across at the shoulder. Say 30 inches for a decent-sized switchback; that's 75 inches one-way.

A chimney with two flues would need to be about six by three as well, or so the book suggested. My first fantasy, you'll remember, had been to have double fireplaces at each end, with exterior stonework. An extravagance, you might say, and you'd be right. But I insisted on a wood-burning stove in the kitchen. Where would that stovepipe go? Clearly wherever the masonry went would affect everything else in the house. The day got hotter, the arguments more intense and closely reasoned. It became obvious that the bill would have to go back to committee or nothing else would get done this session. It was so moved, without dissent. Again, correcting legislation could be enacted later.

In the event, the staircase and the chimney share the hole in the floor reserved for the former, at the expense of that easy-flowing stair. One does not take my risers two at a time. The interior column of brick, though it may not be in precisely the right place, gives the big room a focus, also receives the smoke from the two stoves. It cost less to build than an outside chimney (it was winter and I'll admit to "having it done"), does no disservice to the exterior lines, or the delicate harmony of N.E. barn aesthetic, etc., etc.

The floor went on the following weekend. I had thought we might be able to hang a ceiling at the same time, that is, working from the top. But it proved too difficult without power. (The idea was to lay composition board on the joists underneath the floor as we went along, nailing from below later, an ingenious plan.) As it was, we were delayed by Skip's obsession for keeping the floor flat. The beams weren't much help in that regard: nature abhors a straight line. As a result this floor rests largely on those narrow paddles paint companies give away to their customers for stirring—in this case a serviceable shim.

If you've never laid a floor, you don't know what you're missing. It's a most gratifying job, fast enough to give instant satisfaction, and in this case not so painstaking as to be dull. We carried the heavy planks to our grillwork of beams, 16-, 14-, and 12-foot lengths. Fitting them together, seeing the tight, even join became a kind of harmony, interrupted as if for emphasis by the occasional discordance requiring special measures: pry-bars, wedges, thumbscrews. (Conform, damn you!) And in back more and more of something to walk on, to dance on, to support a brass band.

There's a part of the floor that bounces a bit, I grant that. We were having trouble with the nails, you see, toenailing in at too great an angle, so the boards had a tendency to lift up. But we were interested only in the total emotional effect, seduced by Progress; such minor inconsistencies were sordid and petty.

The nightmare was that we might run out. I counted lumber by moonlight. The next day we wrestled with planks that were warped beyond ordinary usefulness. As we neared the end it was obvious that we weren't going to come out even in any case. Over forty feet you'd have to expect some variation, perhaps just as an accumulation of differences in the joints. In our case more likely due to incompetence. Time to face the music, take out the long tape, do the diagonals. A C minus perhaps; maybe, given the circumstances, a C plus—our rectangle was almost two inches out of square. How come? I don't know. The profane influence of so much travel perhaps. We would wait until the power came in to rip down the final lopsided piece of flooring. In the meantime I tried not to worry about it, congratulating myself instead on the fact that there were but three short lengths left over, or about fifteen dollars worth. On that aspect an A minus, I think.

It was now the last weekend in August. Wife, son, and stepdaughter had returned. They came to see how it was here, now that the cement had set, so to speak. But there was no happening that they could be a part of, and they left for the Cape, almost before I knew what had been decided. It is hard for me to think, to let up, to be emotionally aware, when my body is concentrating on hitting the nail on its head. Perhaps I was beastly then, I don't know.

I called the Barnmover to tell him that it was his turn now. He said, fine, glad you called, can't get there for a week, ten days at the most. Well, good. We draped our bandstand in the sky with plastic, and followed to the coast.

*   *   *

Sand, the open sky, the horizon that stretches for miles and exhausts the mind's eye, blue and blue forming the inseparable bond, the perfect tongue and groove. It is/was my hometown; my childhood is recognizable at every turn of the road to the beach. I remember a lot of people about. Skip, with his friend who was older, and whom he loved, though she seemed indifferent. We were all unfathomable in the ordinary way.

On a beautiful day in late August, facing the sagacious Atlantic, what does it matter? To a boy it is necessary to come between the meeting of the ocean and sand while adults watch behind masks of carefully restrained appreciation. He totters on the edge of immortality, not surprised to be knocked down. It is part of his role as mediator. Perhaps he is asking to be taken back to the sea, I think; or he is learning the secrets of Atlantis from the elegant hiss of the waves as they run over his tiny, delighted feet.

Later his mother and I sat on top of a dune. People we knew and didn't know were milling about on the beach. In a while everyone would have hamburger grilled in a crust of disintegrated rock (good for the lower intestine), and hope to watch the moon come up. It was plain that our courses had parted. It wasn't that she didn't like what I was doing, couldn't see that I was engaged in something important to me. But it was so exclusively mine: what was her part? Did she want a part? She said so, but it would require a 50 per cent interest to find out if that were true. My sense of how it is possible for people to share a life was assaulted at its roots. The land is not mine, no matter what the law says, only the right to occupy it. I was being told that my wife did not trust my occupation, my control. Is that not a sign that the community in which marriage conducts itself is sick unto death? Or is she saying that ownership, that illegitimate idea, has an appeal all its own, independent of our promises to each other? (Sea and sky merge in purple haze at the horizon: but that's a lie. They are separate elements. The illusion creates a ball of emptiness in the center of my self, just below the navel.)

She walked down toward the water's edge, the sand cascading into her footsteps. Soon she was a small figure moving along the beach. I remember thinking: We have come through, but I can't remember through what or what it was supposed to be like on the other—presumably this—side.

In New York, in an office where no matter how often the phone rang it seemed as if nothing was happening, the late summer heat ate oxygen, skyscrapers melting into the sidewalk. The morning's mail brought a letter which said that my mortgage application would not be recommended. One road to the property they found "inaccessible," and the other "a rather rough dirt road with an uneven approach."

My God; the place really was in the country: the Mothering Boonies. The letter went on, if there were another "more accessible" road, it said, "it will be necessary to take the committee by that route."

What was the code? That cement foundation, the

camp under the spruce, the beer in the bottom of the well—perhaps none of it was there after all. Squint only slightly and one could see huge carpenter ants crawling up the walls of Manhattan. Nothing is as it seems.

But surely there is an explanation. The first paragraph is the work of a man who is not particularly happy with his correspondent. In the second he relents. Revelation! It was a wet, miserable day and they got terribly lost! Oh God. Profuse apologies over the phone for the labyrinth of roads, the lack of a competent road crew, mention of neighbors, the friends who knew the lawyer who had connections with the bank. (*They* had been there, without once having to confront the Minotaur.) Well, yes, they would try again, perhaps that very week.

Was there just the hint of a smile in his voice? Was the vice-president really a man of subtle humors and practical jokes? It was something to ponder, and while I was at it, what about the damn building permit?

Again the phone: But hadn't I received the permit last June? Signed? But I was told . . . It seemed, however, that the Certificate of Compliance in accordance with the provisions of Article XI of The State Sanitary Code had been filed. That's it? Somehow I had imagined a different sort of bureaucracy, people to bribe, halls to walk, sweating. It had been done while my back was turned. But, did they have a . . . ah . . . copy of the, what is it called, the building ordinances?

One came in the mail. It said: One-acre plots with 150 feet of accepted roadway; No trailers; $20 fine for each offense. *Uses prohibited:* Dumping of refuse; Distillation of bones; Glue manufacture; Commercial slaughtering; Storage of ash. And then: "The accumulation, harboring or dismantling for sale of metals, automobiles, vehicles or assorted items in a state of disrepair, otherwise known as junk."

There must have been a high-pressure area stalled over the northeast that autumn. August had been dry and mild; September was content to follow. Had the weather turned, I hate to think what disasters might have overtaken us. This September the rain flows off the roof so copiously it is being piped into the field so that erosion doesn't tumble the house head-over-heels down the hill, into the woods. The drainpipe sends out a signal so much like a pot of soup boiling on the wood stove that the absence of a matching aroma confuses the senses.

Already the flowering hawthorne in front of the south window is ripening its fruit. (The thorns make excellent toothpicks, but bite off the sharp point first.) A large yellow maple leaf swings slowly to the ground. There are bluejays in the beeches. This fall will be yellow and gold. At dusk, as the sun sends a brief ray under the cloud, each leaf seems edged with silver.

The dryness of that previous autumn produced a covering frame of orange and red; sunny days, and nights we tried to pretend weren't cold. It was the middle of the week and near dark as I walked across the dewy field from the road, incongruously carrying a bag of groceries and feeling out the newly worn path with my feet. Was something, someone there in that refrigerated, protective swamp? The fire revealed itself first, and then Skip, the bearded wizard of calibration himself, almost sitting on it. He was eating corn, which the garden supplied that first summer with amazing prolificacy. The fire wasn't doing well; he was feeding it leftovers. The cobs burned eventually, he reasoned; if the rhythm was right they would keep the water boiling in the corn pot—and, presto, he had invented a kind of perpetual motion.

Warm sleeping bag, sun coming through the door of the tent; only the promise of self-approval prevented me from rolling over in wonderful luxury. And when we got up to the house, I wished I had stood in the sack: water had gotten under the plastic, condensation maybe. The plastic had heated it up nicely, and the floorboards had swollen and warped, little mountain ranges, wet enough to have formed puddles in places. The plastic was obviously a mistake: better the planks should get wet and dry out in a natural way, we decided, driving down to the store for coffee, doughnuts and a container of orange juice.

While visiting civilization we called the Barnmover. He had said he'd be here, I told his wife, trying to sound firm but friendly. As you might guess, she had no idea, couldn't guess what he was up to, but knew he was planning on coming over. Damn. Every day, every hour was precious: winter would come; that was as certain as taxes. There was so much to do. The well was nearly dry. The electric company was dawdling. The new floor would grow mold before a roof got on it.

We spent some time stacking our old lumber, dragging away brush, keeping busy. Skip would stud in the downstairs walls using the old 3×4's, make a perfect pest of himself with the Juicers—as he called the Electric Company. (We needed all the help we could get.) I had to return to the city.

The omens on the highway weren't any better—a long red slash of blood, on and on, terminating in an awful mess of bones and meat: large dog, I guess, but big enough to be . . . No, didn't I catch a glimpse of fur? It's no good going seventy miles per hour; we weren't meant to travel up and down Her Queendom in this fashion. Drive on, nevertheless, make it pay. Then, while I am in a trance, the Bronx rears up and traps me. Some sort of detour, and stupid with a sleepiness I've made a wrong turn.

The thing is, one step at a time. I had wanted to work with the Barnmover, but it simply wouldn't be possible. I went back up a couple of days later. The Barnmover's big red cherry-picker was parked there in the field, its arm folded like the broken wing of a prehistoric bird. Several posts were in place. And the northernmost roof truss! The rest of the barn was piled up in no order whatsoever, no more prepossessing than the first time I'd seen it laid out.

Still, by the grace of the erratic gods of our fathers something was growing: progress had arrived at Wish-fulfillment Farm. The Man himself arrived in the morning, bounding out of the cab of his truck: "Well, now, how do ya like it so far?" And before I could answer, "Ya just wait, see what we do for ya today." Shortly a car of uncertain vintage drove down the track carrying his two helpers. They had broken training the night before, neither one seemed to be able to open his eyes to the sunlight, or lift his mouth from the carton of coffee he carried. They were sent right up to the front lines nevertheless, complaining bleakly. The Man laughed and announced that he would teach them a lesson, once and for all. He worked the cherry-picker. He said he usta do it all by hand, you know, the way the old guys did. "This here's some faster."

He would fit a section together on the ground, then lift it into place. The rafters were pegged at their peaks, cross-braced with a piece of 2×4 or whatever was handy, and lifted in a unit (the barn has no rooftree) to be set down in their double-notched seat and then *spiked* to the sills. The purist in me rebelled. Our agreement was that everything would be put back the way it had come out; could I justifiably ask that the holes be repegged? There was no shortage of the old oaken pegs, a whole pailful sat on the floor. But I wouldn't be asking him, I'd be asking the kids up there, shirttales hanging out, gasping for breath. I'd let it go for now, I thought.

Skip had painstakingly completed about half the studding downstairs, sawing by hand. We continued, but using a small generator that had come along in the truck. The Man's rotary saw that went along with it had no trigger, for some reason. Just let it run, The Man said. Between the two machines and the Barnmover's chainsaw, with which he cut everything, no matter how big or small, the din was hellish. The carbon monoxide, from what must have been the two dirtiest internal combustion engines ever, drifted slowly to leeward, then was sucked back under the floor, wreathing itself around our heads.

So we cut as many of the studs as we could manage and mutually decided to turn the abominable generator off. What a price to pay for efficiency! (Is it efficient to be so discomforted?) Such noise disfigures the very landscape, as if some alien fluid had found a way into the fibers of living things, under the soil and through the rock. Only when the reverberations died away were common shapes resumed. The Swedish crosscut is sharp and does a good job if you don't try to press it. It makes a sound like a saw in a comic strip. Skip's hammer is sure, the head striking the nail rhythmically—now we sound like carpenters.

At lunchtime The Man disappeared in the helper's car. They'd not brought lunch. He returned from the general store with an armload of canned beef stew, crackers, cookies, milk. A fire was made, and I believe even the darkest, most distraught of them had a reasonably good meal of it, eating out of the tins. I knew what I was paying to get this frame up, and I knew those guys couldn't be getting rich, especially if'n they were drinkin' store-bought booze.

The Barnmover had a way of keeping them going; his strength was a matter of pride to them, and in turn he was constantly exhorting them not to take chances "up there." How do you not take a chance when one of these huge beams comes swinging around, dangling from the end of the crane and you are balanced on an 8×8 twenty feet up. And talk about chainsaw cowboys: he had a big old Stihl, if I'm remembering right. To start it he would hold it out in front of him with one hand, pulling the starting rope with the other. (While he was off collecting lunch I tried the same method, to the amusement of the assembled crew. I think I could have just about managed with some training, but only if I grew another arm—I couldn't even hold it up one-handed!)

One of the four crossbeams needed mending. It's approximately $14'' \times 16''$ of rock-hard chestnut, but the constant wet under the mysterious dormer had withered it at the joint. (Chestnut is the most durable of woods; it rotted in this instance I'm sure only because of the intrusion of the less resistant oak tenon. Once the North American woods were rich in chestnut, but an Asian fungus wiped them out in the first decades of this century —another victim of international commerce.) The post underneath is a replacement, the only column not fluted, the whole held up then by braces. I could see why it was easier to do this sort of thing in place: standing on a platform above the beam, the man lopped off the mangled end, then cut a long tenon in what remained. On the ground a piece of oak beam imported for the purpose and even wider than the chestnut was cut to fit, with a mortise for the crossbeam and another to receive the rafter coming down. But the rafter tenon had rotted as well, so a new one was made by fitting in what I guess you'd have to call a double-ended tenon. The joining required much levering, shouting, considerable work with a sledge hammer, "the persuader" he called it. Once the splice was made, three holes were drilled through the joint for the pegs. All of this was done with a kind of brutal accuracy—nothing had to be cut twice— a simplicity (not to mention efficiency) that would have made the original builders believe they were watching men from a different planet.

In fact, that splice has dropped a trifle now, and I will shortly fasten onto its face a piece of one-fourth-inch steel strap, $4'' \times 48''$, using large lag screws and my new rachetted socket wrench, this just so that that corner of my mind can be liberated to worry about something else; and because I will enjoy doing it, enjoy having the right materials, the right tools.

At the time the major worry was the bank. If they were just stalling, figuring out a good reason for saying no, I was in a terrible fix. As a child I used to look forward to driving by a particular field not far from home; down in a small hollow was a half-built house, bare wooden walls on a stone foundation, half a dozen rafters, no windows. The nails rusted and made a pleasing pattern on the boards. The whole slowly turned grey, cracking open as if needing to let something out. What awful tragedy was represented by this dream dying so publicly in winter rain, summer sun? Now, alas, I knew; the mortgage hadn't happened! Of course, it would take a lot longer for this structure to collapse; thus it would do so even more publicly. And what a folly it would seem as it succumbed to the inevitable subaerial destruction!

Could one call up the vice-president and say; Look, I have this disturbing memory from my childhood, and I really need to know what you're going to do? Perhaps you could be that free; but I am too old, and cynicism, that most crippling disease, won't allow me to believe anything would be accomplished by such an extravagant gesture.

So far I had spent over $16,500:

$10,000	downpayment for the land
2,000	Barnmover
2,240	Mr. Louie
750	septic tank and backfill
82	beams
1,512	floorboards

The tools and other incidentals (camping equipment, fencing) I counted as out-of-pocket expenses, and I tried to say they didn't count. I was, therefore, more than $4,000 in debt, and when the Barnmover finished I would have to come up with another $4,000. At the time I figured the roof and siding would cost $3,000. So a minimum of $11,000 was still needed to close in. It would shut the project down if I had to apply over again to another bank; and then—blow blow, thou winter's wind, thou art not so unkind as man's inability to recognize a good financial risk.

The Barnmover said, "Just you get a roof on it, tack some paper down. Anyway, you got lotsa time. I've been up on roofs like that there middle of winter." And in his shirt-sleeves, I thought, a hammer in each hand, spitting roofing nails.

Yes, whatever else happened a roof was imperative. Early that morning, the roof timbers almost in place, Skip and I went off to the Lumber Yard, the one I had established as being no more expensive, and the most helpful, of those that delivered. (I had already charged $787.94 worth of 2×4's, 2×6's, nails, plyscore, plastic sheeting, etc.) Crowded on a Friday morning, the office a frame structure meant to show off the materials used to build it: a modified colonial ranch in the style of a country store. A short counter with stools among samples of building gadgetry: window sashes and wrought-iron hardware. You wait while the man in front of you explains his problem with the sliding closet door, or a roofer figures out with the help of the salesman's computer how many squares of shingles he needs. Any show of impatience is as welcome as a turd at a dog show, for here no problem exists that can't be solved by something, or someone who's done it before; it requires only the quiet, respectful approach.

I am advised that a 1×6 spruce, tongue-and-grove, is about the cheapest roof sheathing I could use, since I've ruled out plyscore on aesthetic grounds. As for insulation, well, Peter, most people these days, for A-frames and such like what you've got, would lay down some rigid polyurethane. Out came the catalogue. It was comforting that someone actually manufactured a product designed to do what we wanted, for a minute it made us feel that we knew what we were doing. But the insulation was for later. We ordered the matched spruce, 2,000 feet of it: 100 sixteen-footers, 100 fourteen-footers, 60 tens and 50 eights, following the advice of this Prince among Pragmatists (later we needed another 40 sixteens: total price $541.70, including the nails to hold it down).

Our friend retired into the back room to use the calculator (but who needs help to find out how much 2,000 feet of lumber costs at $230 per thousand?) and have a word with The Chief Prince. I said something to Skip, something workmanlike and responsible, while watching the tone of the brief discussion. Glances through the open door. The order is written up. As I sign it the Prince manages somehow to imply that mortgage money is hard to find these days. And I say yes, isn't it, and I was talking to the Veep at the Cozy Cottage Bank just a few days ago. And he asks if I was doing business with them. And I say I *thought* so. And that is the end of it.

While we had the man's full attention it seemed a good idea to talk about siding. What did he think of buying green hemlock? (What would he think, since they don't sell such; but it's always good to hear a pitch by someone who knows what he's about.) We went back out into the yard. They had just unloaded a boxcar of Western cedar, 1×12; rough-sawn, it was very nearly its nominal size. They were selling a lot of it. Easy to work with; and you'll never have to paint it, Peter, just let it weather naturally; $490 a thousand, more than double the cost of Brand X, but so much less work. How much would we need? Well, it seemed they had a guy who was a whiz at calculating how much and in what lengths to minimize waste. They'd send him over, no obligation. (No obligation, no cash. What a nice way to do business, though I can't help wondering if they sprang to the phone the minute we were out of the office. If so, the Veep must have been kind.)

The studs were all up downstairs; we just needed a piece of floor to sleep on and the camp could be struck, provided it didn't rain. We started nailing a grid of 2 × 6's (18″ on center, crossbraced every 24″) covering the long-standing puddle. There were frogs in it, I noticed as we started to work. With the floor overhead and the mud underneath, it was dark and unpleasant. And because of my stupidity with the early planning, and the shorter foundation, the floor we were working on was below the granite outcropping at the other end. We were planning a step as a result, thus cutting overhead clearance to zero for anyone over six feet tall.

The Barnmover stuck his head and shoulders through the stair hole, peering into the gloom. "Don't save on nails," he said. Then lowering himself down a makeshift ladder he gave us the benefit of his experience. "You guys got a bit of a problem here, ain'tcha? I tell ya, if it was mine, 'course it ain't and there are all kinds of ways, but if it was mine I'd pour the sonovabitch." (Pause) "Sure. Get that crazy guy back here with them cement trucks. Pour some concrete. Won't cost any more and be a helluva lot quicker."

Well, he was dead right, and I had been trying my best to avoid the same train of thought. It was my natural aversion to cement that had gotten in the way. A partial cement floor would make it possible to keep to one level in back, though the rock still would be just about poking through the floor; it would save us time, and I could have him pour the floor for my secret fantasy, a double-sized shower with three shower heads, round and lined in wood like the inside of a huge barrel. (Actually it has only two shower heads, which turn out to be plenty—and making a round interior was too much trouble. It is lined in cedar, however, and in the otherwise Spartan interior is thought to be quite luxurious.)

As this discussion dragged on, as they are wont to do in any boardroom, the lumber truck appeared, cautiously making the dangerous turn. I was glad to find the truckers interested in what was happening, admiring of the view, and I thought in turn to lend a hand in unloading. But by his example Skip gave me to understand that the convention did not require it, indeed there were some union work rules governing that sort of thing. Time is money . . . or, more importantly, money is time.

Time, the season passing, that realization of summer as immediate history. The field had turned yellow while we were looking elsewhere, at bankbooks or white lines on asphalt. The blueberry bushes contributed a spot of red. The camp was cold, and no matter how the fire might be stoked, the night air crept under your jeans, pressed unwelcome fingers along your backbone. Washing was an act of special courage that often found us wanting. (At a market I asked for a box to tote the groceries in, explaining that there was no driveway. The young woman looked at me with some interest and asked, "Where do you live, anyway?" in a tone that made me aware of just how much I reeked of apple smoke, chain-saw exhaust, sweat. It figures that she wouldn't be found smelling of anything not sold by her employers. But if her employers really want to get rich they should put out an odor that is as inescapably unhygienic as we were then: call it Campfire Cologne, for Men and Women.)

Despite my frantic impatience, I suppose things were moving as fast as could be expected. The frame was nearly finished, still a singularly unimpressive skeleton, just a lot of old wood variously held together. The electric company had completed their survey, and I had signed the agreement that would allow them to put a pole down: we would have only to dig a trench for the cable to hook up temporary service. (No extra charge for the poles, but a guarantee of at least $180 per annum in fees.) That week Louie came over and gave me a price by phone. It was probably too much, but was I going to argue? He would get some men over to grade the following weekend.

The next Friday, the Inaugural Weekend, all the elder children came on the bus, the first time since their indolent summer vacations. It was cold and clear; we ate quickly in town, wanting to arrange some sort of camp before dark. It was not going to be cozy. With some misgivings, we built a fire inside the foundation: the smoke exited through the basement window opening as long as the wind cooperated. We were all hobos huddled under a railroad bridge, the night beyond endlessly hostile. The train hooted in the valley, finding us out. Everyone had brought his own sleeping bag, but six people take up a lot of room, and we were short of floor space. Daddy slept—or didn't sleep—on a ledge over a precipice, the sleeping bag trailing in the mud under our platform.

I lay awake unnerved by circumstances, grateful for children so amazingly game. Soon there would be beds, water, popcorn and hot cocoa. In the meantime we learn. Yes, and sleep. But I had only dozed off when I was awakened by a footstep—a rustling of dead leaves. Quiet, then another step, then two more in rapid succession. I sat up. The bare studs make an unpleasant pattern against the blue-black sky. The marauder was inside now, and I wasn't the only person who had heard him. My oldest child said, "What's that?" And I said, "It's a skunk, of course, go back to sleep." But the skunk found us attractive; or was it the eggs stored under some lumber? I suggested quietly that we let it have its way; having walked over the bottom of my sleeping bag, it seemed content to travel on.

A few minutes later it was back; now everyone was up, and Skip lit the kerosene lantern. He was of the opinion that they don't like light, since they always stayed a certain distance from the campfire down the hill. I got up, advancing on a very healthy, rude animal, who had indeed found the stash of groceries fifteen feet away. He made no acknowledgment whatever of my presence. After some indecision, a kind of dance—back and forth—it seemed the better part of valor to hang the light from a nail on one of the studs, returning to my precipice. The position of both parties was thus improved: the dull glow cast by the lantern identified his dinner (our breakfast) for our friend, *and* it had the effect of making us feel much more secure. Some might think the skunk got the better of the deal, and they'd be right. Skunks generally do.

VII

Knee-deep in Hubris

"For my panacea, instead of one of those quack vials of a mixture dipped from Acheron and the Dead Sea . . . let me have a draught of undiluted morning air! If men will not drink of this at the fountainhead of the day, why then, we must bottle up some and sell it in the shops, for the benefit of those who have lost their subscription ticket to the morning time in this world . . ." Thus the Preacher of Walden shows his versatility; no doubt he would have made a superb adman. The spot continues: "Remember, it will not keep quite till noonday even in the coolest cellar . . ." and the camera pulls back on the New England farmhouse at dawn, the product superimposed . . .

Lost your subscription? Had you routed yourself from

your warm sleeping bag that morning (not as hard as sometimes for the one who had volunteered to do without the foam-rubber pad and had anyway spent the night waking to every noise, as if in a combat zone), while emptying your bladder and warming your joints you would have watched the eastern sky ripening until the horizon itself was ignescent. And then an awesome bursting of light like molten steel, an alchemy hidden in its brightness. The colors of the forest—scarlet and orange, blood-red, gold—are reduced to mild halftones. You would see each drop of moisture in a wet landscape infused with light, sequins; the mist below lifting, slowly, drawn up as by the magician's sword. But listen, the noise you hear is water in joyful pursuit of itself down the valley, *only* that; or rather only that and its interior echo —the pulse of blood through strengthening flesh, sparks in the brain remembering the blackness of the cave and the rhythms of the rockfire, the now-done darkness.

Early rising may be a moral virtue—but it is of sure practical value. We needed each of these days, needed the clear sky and the still-lingering afternoons. The demands of earning a living required my presence in the city five days a week, though I could shave it to four in emergencies. And by the Grace of the Gods (everything is possible at six o'clock) we would have this place closed in and heatable by Thanksgiving. (To be specific—something I avoided as much as possible—that meant getting some plumbing in, a toilet and a cold-water tap, insulation in all the exterior walls, a modicum of electricity and perhaps an electric heater. Also a fireplace. Asking too much? Well, look, just a few weeks before there was *nothing* here at all . . .)

The Barnmover's red cherry-picker was still parked in front of the brave, bare skeleton of beams. The week previous it had broken down, something to do with the hydraulic system; it sat listing slightly to starboard, its wing half poised for flight. He would be back to fix it and clean up early this morning. Time to rout out the troops. Hit the deck! Feet on the floor! (What floor? a small figure asks, sleepily, crossly.) This camp is the worst equipped of them all. Water is farther away, there is no means to hold a pot over the fire, it is damp (though warmer than the valley). For washing I tried to start a march on the creek. Down there a couple of hundred yards through the evergreens was the tub I had made, a dam of rocks where the banks were clear. The trick was to run down, tearing off clothes as you approached. It wasn't cold then until you got to shucking the sneakers. In fact, I found it invigorating to be naked at the edge of that small stream, in a forest of evergreens reaching up and cradling in all at the same time; it seemed no colder with clothes off than on. Others did not always agree.

The real test came when it was necessary actually to get yourself to interrupt the water in its course. The moss-covered rocks were indeed cold, and slippery: care had to be taken just when the instinct was to throw the body in. In what? The tub wasn't more than two feet deep and only just long enough to allow me to stretch out. After a good rain—there hadn't been any recently

—there was room enough to float. But oh what cleanliness was available there, the pores flushed and the skin washed inside and out. There with the sun just coming through the trees, watching the tiny water skimmers as I stood on the edge of the pool, dripping, I thought, no matter how civilized this place might get, I must always come down here once in a while to bathe. Alas, a hot shower is so much easier to arrange, to make time for; I fear progress has run off with another intention for moral improvement.

But children don't need moral improvement, and Skip was too thin to risk being cold; anyway he thought his enveloping aroma protective, warming, and perhaps he was right.

Now, about this roof. Do you start from the top and work down? No, because then you have nothing to work on, dopey. Okay, then, where do you start? There must have been some kind of overhang on these eaves but the original rafter ends had largely decayed, and unevenly. The Barnmover was under his crane whacking at something with a hammer. He heard us nonetheless, pulled himself up and suggested we make some false rafter ends out of 2×6's (we could always trim them off later), and toenail them into the wall-plate. That meant cutting eleven fittings, I counted, twenty-two hand sawings for each side. A long chore, most of the morning. Not at all, said the man. Stand back, fellas. And so he figured the angle with his floor square, cut a stereotype with his handy chainsaw. Was it right? Skip took it up the ladder and we all looked, as if we were hanging a new painting.

Shorter, I thought. Nah, said the Barnman. Shorter, I said, asking Skip for his view. He wasn't sure, so we changed places. The children were asked. Conservative to the end, the eldest wondered what the roof had been like before. Ah, yes; shorter then.

We had a lot of ends from the basement floor. These were piled up, one on top of the other, the pattern topmost, and our resident Bunyan sliced down the pile as if cutting through so many griddle cakes with a knife. Six at a time, the lot was cut in a few minutes. It took us longer to tack them onto the plate. That done, we snapped the chalked line along them, holding the ends of the line as near as possible to the exact corners. The first of the matched spruce would be nailed along that line, presumably even.

But before we could really get working we had to build a scaffolding along the wall: again, 2×6's (for some reason they cost no more than 2×4's that year) nailed securely to the wall posts, braced at a 45-degree angle. I got three 12-penny double-headed nails into each joining of brace and post. Skip came along and put in two more. "You kill yourself, it's okay," he said, "it's your house. But I don't take chances."

So here goes the first board, only I don't know where the roof ends. I ask if an eight-inch overlap at the gable ends is about right. About there? More? A foot, it's decided; the nails go through into the rafters.

Now another problem. We thought the roof was going to be 40 feet long, thus lengths of 16, 14, and 10 feet. But the roof is 42 feet long with the overhang. We really need a 17 and an 11 on each end, as it would be good to have these boards abut at the major rafters. Back to the yard? But it's deemed not necessary; we go with what we've got, particularly since it might be a good thing, we rationalize, to stagger the joints.

Once the bottom edge is on, we try to find a working rhythm. For a while the Barnman and a helper work with us, he showing us that it is easier joining if you nail the bottom edge of the planks first, then fit in the groove of the next, nailing the top of one and the bottom of the new, and on and on. The surface begins to grow. The kids pass the lumber up to us, and soon I'm up on the roof itself. "Next!" The four of us can just about keep up with the supply, leaving the ends ragged so that we don't have to cut to size. They'll be trimmed when there's power. (It bothers me that this way of doing it is so much like something I would have done as a child: *then* it would never have been finished.)

But soon the Barnmover had to remind himself that he was not being paid to be a carpenter. He had only to fit in the heavy purlin on the other, west side of the roof. This was the member stretched between the major rafters, adding support to the lesser rafters. I had thought to build a dormer on that side, making it possible to have a real room upstairs with a view of the sun setting over a distant ridge. But to do so meant either cutting that purlin or moving it higher to allow clearance to anyone approaching the dormer window. (It *could* just be left there, the dormer built with a floor at that height, a smaller window, and the whole thing a sleeping platform lined in foam rubber. I think: we would regret that after the fact.) The engineering necessary for moving that purlin wasn't even challenging, as it turned out. The real problem other than time was my ambivalence about altering this grand old antique, like putting an innerspring in an old rope bed. It is more comfortable, but anyone can sleep on an innerspring.

Well, do you or don't you? 'cause it gotta be now if you do. In the end all it took was the intention; a couple of new mortises were cut, by the helper—slowly and carefully. I had the idea that he rather liked standing in one place, in the glorious sun, looking over the valley. Cleverly the old joints were used for the knee-braces, the crane was driven around to the side, and with the earnest help of the gentle persuader the job was done by lunch. You wouldn't know the difference if I hadn't told you, either, though you would see that the dormer itself had been framed by an amateur.

On our side the roof was less than a quarter done, but we had been building it from the northeast corner, and from underneath it already looked like something like a barn roof. The rafters soared higher, the crossbeams were heavier, more stately, the slender bracing became the continuity, the grammar, that held reason together.

But it wouldn't do to spend time looking. Three more days to finish the sheathing at this rate; half a day added on account of framing the dormer, and another half to cover with the felt. We'd be into the third weekend before the skin could go on. I wanted metal roofing, but I didn't want to ask the Yard to order it before the bank was heard from. And more in desperation than as the result of careful study, a decision had been made in favor of the cedar siding. I was only waiting for the man to tell us how much was needed. That would be over a thousand anyway ($1,205.55, in fact). And there was the $325 for the cement floor. It was late September, still hot working in the sun. If it was to be the middle of October before the roof was finished . . .

It was all possible, barring interruptions and acts of God. But the artificial press of time affected the work. That morning I had found a patch of rafter that was rotten. There was good wood on the under side, it wasn't —according to the expert—significantly weakened, but it wouldn't hold onto the nail. I had to chop out the bad wood, laying in a piece of furring. It was the right way to cope, but how I resented the ten, fifteen minutes it consumed. And in the back of the head always the dog on the highway, and the voice saying that if it is worth doing, it's worth doing right.

We had the man from the lumber yard with us that weekend, I believe. I only remember his walking about the place, asking us for the dimensions, a heavyset man in white overalls with no visible means of computing. You say, What's the big deal, once you know the dimensions? The deal is that the lumber cost near One Dollar, U.S., for every two feet, over four cents an inch. So you don't want to have to cut off a lot of short useless ends. It makes good kindling, but at that price?

I followed the guy around, explaining that the siding would be applied separately to the downstairs and the north and south sides, overlapping at the gable line. What about battens? I thought we'd batten from the inside, I explained, using spruce. (Battens cover the seams between the boards, but if you cover in from the inside, there's an extra ¾ inch of dead space [i.e. insulation], you have a flush exterior, and the battens can be cheaper, since they're not exposed.)

I watched the response. "That'll save you some money," he said with just a hint of approval. On Monday, Skip took delivery of 19 twenty-two-foot lengths, of 1 × 12 cedar siding (rough-sawn), 15 eighteens, 5 sixteens and 112 twelves, as well as 200 feet of 1 × 3's and 20 pounds of nails. Later we needed another 40 twelves ($235.10 worth—less than $1,500 for all the siding).

Sunday morning Louie showed up with two of his crew, tall angular men. With their tools carried over their shoulders they seemed right out of Goya as they walked in from the road. Perhaps they were the same lads who had been asleep in the cab that day long before. But they weren't lads, and when we offered them a beer (the stash now rested on the bottom of the old well near the road) they looked embarrassed and shook their heads.

The afternoon's work on the roof hardly seemed to make any difference. We were off the scaffolding but had run into trouble because of the sublime curvature of the old beams. Over the largest bay the rafters had bent, under the weight of time perhaps, as much as three or four inches. The planks could easily follow that bend, but the result, of course, was that a gap developed. Thus I had to rip down sixteen feet of plank by hand. A sharp saw, a reasonably solid surface to work on—the stack of wood—something else to think about so as not to extend the tool. It takes only a few minutes, but my arm is not used to it, and the knowledge of the electric saw's great speed makes this expenditure of energy onerous. There's a different smell to hand work, however; I believe the wood remains more pungent, wetter, the smell of the wood-working shop in grade school. (For a year of my life it was the only class I looked forward to; why was I so bad at it? Why did I never get anything done? Or did I only like the smell?)

Meanwhile Skip made us a ladder of 2 × 4's, since the Barnmover's gear, including his ladder, would depart on the morrow. (The generator had long since disappeared, as if by general consent.) He didn't spare the nails, strong rungs but not too many, figuring in his calculating way that the fewer steps, the faster up and down.

Yes, we could have corrected the wavy roof line, either by turning the offending member inside out and waiting for gravity to effect an adjustment or, had time been available, by filling in the roof side of the bent beams. But why? The roof is very nearly a 45-degree slope; an even edge wouldn't make it any more rainproof. It looks now as if it had melted slightly in the sun, or in winter as if the weight of the snow had pressed it in. I believe that it's solid; I like the questions it raises. In fact, it's my view that the rigid geometric pattern of twentieth-century building is a uniform bore. Look at the engravings of the seventeenth and eighteenth centuries, the fenceposts that have given way to the constant pressure of the earth's shifting mantle, the pleasing roundness of a thatched roof. There is much that is pleasing in irregularity, in building as in humankind.

The two dirt rakers were finished; we saw them walking to the road to be picked up. When they were out of earshot Skip said that he didn't believe they could speak English; perhaps they were relatives of the boss? No doubt they are sending all their money home, wherever that might be. Perhaps they couldn't be making very much? At least that might explain the unusual dependence, the lack of transport. So, the American dream lives in the backwoods despite all. Hurray! Soon the cement trucks and highway graders will be emblazoned with the names of these newcomers from the Pyrenees, or Croatia, or wherever.

In the months spent crisscrossing the countryside in search of a nest, there was one junk store that kept appearing by the side of the road. Sometimes it seemed as if it were following me around. Often enough there was something interesting on its weathered, ragged porch. In order to break the spell I went into it one day; there had been a nice wood-burning parlor stove in the back room. Perhaps it was there still. A stove of some sort would soon be a necessity in that downstairs quasi-room, and most parlor stoves can double as a cooking tool.

The guy knew I was coming—I mean, he must have had some sort of premonition. There was even a sign propped up against the highway fence: "Wood Stoves." Of course, that sort of thing is unheard-of now; since the so-called oil crisis any one who put up a sign like that would have to be carried away after the riot. There were, in fact, three wood-burning kitchen stoves on the porch. One was enamel, I remember, and one couldn't quite manage to differentiate itself from the bureau that had only two of its four drawers, or the thirties metal bedside table, the broken grindstone and the several milk cans standing in a row. But this other was a black stove, staunch and sturdy, hard-working, with some rust on the top and a sound oven below, the classic bulbous base and curved feet, nickel-plated trim and warming shelf. The firebox and its grates were intact, but the round burner covers didn't seem to fit too well, and on the top there were gaps where the different parts should, presumably, be tight. Still, the oven door said loudly "STANDARD G" and, underneath, "Somerworth Foundry, Salmon Falls, N.H." As far as I was concerned, it was a gift from Prometheus himself.

I tried the door of the shop. It was locked, though someone/thing was moving around inside. I knocked again, then stepped back in a show of innocence. A lock squeaked; the old man was sorry, there had been robberies, you couldn't be too careful.

What? A hundred and ten dollars? (He must have been watching my inspection.) They was selling in the fancy stores for a lot more than that, he said. Were they really? (Maybe he's right, there couldn't be many more like this around. I had been expecting to pay perhaps $30 or $40. Could I say $60?) I was thinking maybe $75, I said. I mean, look at this rust. We haggled some. He said it had been in constant use till just a little while ago and he wouldn't go below $90. Okay, but he had to include a poker with a nickel handle, an extra cover, a wrench to shake down the ashes, an iron pot.

By all accounts that was one of the most spectacular autumns for a long time. The next three weekends it seemed as if Isis had banished the clouds from the sky forever. There certainly could not have been a finer backdrop for my obsession nor a richer gift, and no prayer of thanksgiving would have been too extravagant in reply had I but known one. (Alas, poor Isis). Had I been rich enough to spend those three weeks hammering away nails instead of selling words, there would have been shelter for the winter without doubt. But it seemed necessary to continue playing a role in each camp, though from this distance it could be argued that the necessity was a device which allowed me to say: Ah, but if only there had been time.

Yes, and there would have been no great dishonor to letting tarpaper keep out the snow for one season. But to have taken that course I would have had to acknowledge during those weeks in early autumn, "Look, this isn't going to be possible." Pride intervened, vanity, the justification of selfish decisions taken, and the compromises leading to estrangement.

Skip knew a guy who was working as a carpenter for a museum in the city. I couldn't pay him enough to make a difference, but perhaps he would count it a lark. Call him Lars—a laconic Squarehead just like me, but with roots in the Midwest. I don't think it could have been done without him; without his example as much as the strength of his arm. He had that certain pace of the completely competent, knowing when to push and when to relax, knowing what is possible and what isn't.

The rest of that twenty-pound box of nails found its way into the roof during the next two days. With the help of a constant, bantering competition we got a lot done. (Hey, you call that straight? Bend one for me, willya? Look, he's *walking!*) Perhaps the others found it a little tiresome at the end of eight hours in the sun, looking at the shiny surface of the spruce, disciplining boards that were often slightly warped, split or had damaged edges. Sheer plod makes plow down sillion/Shine, said the poet; and yes, look at the sun pour off this glossy, embered surface, highlights dancing like half-seen elves on the swoop and buckle of the aged ribs. The ragged ends needed only cutting off and the barn was whole again, breathing again, albeit shallowly.

In my memory the sequence is filmed double time, with the camera lingering on the finished roof at the end, fading . . . But the gods know it was not a job that required great precision; the one difficulty was keeping to a straight line, end to end, and if you'll study the ceiling now, you'll see that we were content to make do where a more professional crew would not have.

Up the east face to the ridge, up the west face, and then rip the boards for the last course. Lars did it in the ancient manner, splitting the planks with a hatchet and then planing to get a reasonably straight edge. Meanwhile the dormer was framed up with half-round rafters the Barnmover had thoughtfully left behind. I had wanted to make a gabled dormer, as would befit the original design, but I feared the skills at my disposal were not up to it. Skip was quick to point out that any dormer was out of keeping; if you're going to be sacrilegious, what matter the severity of the words you choose. As resident rationalizer there was obviously none better than he, and there was no way to deny the logical conclusion: it would be a shed roof. There's a relief.

The rafters were notched to sit on the moved purlin, four of them, the eye said, would do it fine for a roof six feet wide. But before we knew how long they should be —without having to do a lot of arithmetic—we would put up the posts and lintel that would form the outside of the dormer wall. The bottoms of these posts stand on the wall-plate: they could be spiked in solidly and would be also held in place by the framing of the dormer itself. I had laid aside some 4×4's earlier, tough old oak, hand-hewn and straight-grained, from where I couldn't remember. Working at them was a delight, and I would have liked to take the time to make a proper joint in the old way. On the other hand, Skip had another saying: If you've got nails, use 'em. So the posts and the lintel were lap-jointed, four simple notchings.

Setting up the posts and stretching the lintel between them was a job that by rights required a hoist of some sort. But where's the time? I would have to perch myself (couldn't ask anyone else to do it—even if someone were willing) on the edge of the world up there, too far from the ground and nothing much to hold on to. It's only a question of balance and will and careful deep breaths to keep in touch with your center: up the impractical ladder with you. The six-foot post is shoved up to me, two random lengths of plank tacked to its inside edges. Now I must set it down, holding it straight with one hand while drawing the hammer from its holster with the other, and take a couple of swipes at the nail which will fix the braces to the rafter. It's a long stretch, one foot on the ladder, knee on the putative dormer sill. I've pulled it over far too much, the nail has to be pulled, the post topples down and over the roof edge. Shit!

But like everything else, it's much easier the second time; I know that I must divide my attention between keeping the post relatively plumb and getting the brace nailed. And I can ask for a little eyeball help from the ground. For the lintel, well, just don't look down: Skip holds onto me belt. It's all strength and keeping the feet planted and don't forget to breathe; lift, feeling the weight in the arms and shoulders, set it down easily. See? Anything's possible; we are all geniuses.

Are you looking at that framing somewhat critically? The posts are the same height, I can assure you, but damn me, I forgot that the plate itself sags off, as if weary of its part in all this. It doesn't affect the view, but as that roof catches quite a lot of rain, and as it all rolls off the north corner, it's best not to have that window open in a rainstorm. (As for the wall-plate, its complaint got rather tiresome, and to shut it up two stout 6×6 chestnut posts from the Home have been called back into service, lending their youthful strength to the proceedings.)

The dormer was sheathed the following weekend, at the end of which we also had the paper down over all the spruce. So now let it rain. The trouble was that the one time it did rain was just after the floor had been poured downstairs, in the middle of the week. Mr. Louie had other jobs, after all. We walked through the unfinished walls, and there in the place of the familiar dirt was real floor. Nice job! Smooth, clean. Flat. Even the shower drain was in the right place. But what are those little holes? They look like ant-traps in the sand. Damn! There's all that plastic sheeting around. You'd think . . . But I should have been here and . . . Does it make much difference in the end? In fact, the concrete is all covered, it's too cold, you know.

Now we had a floor and a ceiling: it remained to put up the outside walls. The cedar lay in thick, rich, aromatic stacks out front, and it was a great relief to see how fast it went. The inside batten first, then the cedar plank nailed through that into the studs or lateral nailers. The next batten would be squeezed in behind the unnailed edge, and so on. The planks were very close to a foot wide (it would take about forty-four to cover the lower west face). We used the twelve-footers, cutting off some fifty-five cents worth on each, to my continuing discomfort. By this time we had invested in a device that magically converted the car's electric system into current that would run a saw. Of course, the car had to be idling when it was used, and at a fairly raucous clip. Only in America: it is certainly the most ferociously wasteful supplier of electrical current ever devised. In fact, we found that the good Swedish crosscut worked almost as fast. But the electricity could be pressed into service for ripping purposes, and it might have saved us a lot of time if I'd thought of it sooner.

Decisions, decisions, decisions. Avoiding them had been a disease with me. Windows? A front door? How to cope with the final stage of roofing? It was the last weekend in September, and no further procrastinations could be allowed. I would even have to call the bank come Monday. The window problem presented the most serious sort of challenge. My first hope had been to find some old factory or mill windows, outsized but preferably mullioned. On closer inspection that idea became patently quixotic. Although the east wall is unfenestrated except for the traditional transom window, the rest of the main floor would be 30 per cent glass, south and west. It ought to be double-glazed, and who wants to build that many storm windows, that many window frames. Insulated glass, then, and windows made to open and shut, for the most part, though I don't have to worry about ventilation: windows high in the gables take care of that.

Reluctantly, I had taken the problem to the Yard. There were advantages to buying new. As soon as such were admitted in evidence, my desire to recycle, be clever, above all be unique was instantly subverted. How cunning these guys are. The windows come in all sizes, welded glass, all the wood work done, just set 'em in to your rough opening and nail 'er down, screens on the inside—on and off in a matter of *minutes.* I was a goner as soon as they handed over the catalogue.

But downstairs? There would be the big bay window facing south: that opening I can cover temporarily with second-hand storm windows, otherwise two big sliding doors. The good ones from the nationally advertised firm cost about $400 *each.* Others from a smaller firm down south, $215, and yes, they are just as good; at least I don't see how the big guy could improve on them $185 worth. The doors had been ordered, but fortunately the windows could wait while the matter was further deliberated. In any case we could get on with studding up the walls, as all the rough-opening sizes were somewhere in the catalogue's small print.

Enough cheap insulation for the roof, in two-inch Styrofoam in sheets $2' \times 8'$, cost $366. The good stuff, two-inch polyurethane with aluminum paper on both sides, cost $585 per thousand square feet. The roof was just over 1,600 square feet, but as the stuff is sold in sheets $4' \times 12'$, we'd better take thirty-four, i.e. $983.36 including tax. Jeeesus. Almost three times Brand X.

The Prince of Pragmatists and your correspondent are eyeball to eyeball over the formica counter. He knows I want to spring for it and is looking for the right button: "Take the cheaper if you want, it will do *almost* as good a job." I am thoughtful; this puts me way over budget. We have already discussed the R ratings, and there is no doubt expensive is better; but how much difference will it make? "Look," he says, his tone ominous as he leans a little closer, "save your money on something else, that Brand X is real shit." He didn't say it as much as he let the word slip through his clenched teeth. Well, okay! (How we respond to plain talk!) I had a pretty good bill going; they wouldn't mind adding it on? But the order was already written.

The roof would be done in the following manner, we decided over beer and pizza: first, a crosshatching of 2×6 laid flat on the roof and nailed firmly into the rafters, this to add strength as well as to provide an inch and a half of dead space as added protection against the hostile elements. The sheets of insulation would be nailed over that, flush; the aluminum roofing (another $400), nailed through the urethane into the 2×6's. That meant of course that the roofing nails would have to be at least two and a half inches long, since the insulation had no holding power whatsoever. Skip argued for laying the insulating panels between the 2×6, but then we'd have to build up the 2×6 a half-inch to make a flush surface, and we'd lose all that nice dead space. I guessed we could find the right nails. But the final two layers would have to go on simultaneously, or nearly so, as we should not risk letting the rain at that synthetic stuff, I had been told—perhaps it would melt, reconstitute itself.

In a city where no one seems to know what is happening just outside the gates, our efforts become heroic and favored of the gods. Look up! Look: the towers point to a cerulean sky, a color so intense just that glimpse must

tell you something of Autumn's protracted and luxurious death, the classic drama played out as few will see
twice in a decade. But the crowds of people walk the
streets with their eyes on their shoes or the closing prices
on The Exchange. That I have lived and sung in your
midst will one day make you illustrious, they murmur to
the curbstones, believing Whitman's wonderful, unbe-
lievable celebration.

I am favored with a letter from the bank. It is opened
with no little trepidation. But it is good news; surely we
are on the right side! The vice-president writes that they
are as pleased as can be to approve the mortgage loan:
$26,000 at 9 per cent, monthly payments of $263.80. Put
another way it costs $21,229.65 to borrow $26,000 for
fifteen years. Of course, I can pay it off early if I get lucky,
but with inflation being what it is, that wouldn't be smart,
I'm told. (But for how long can we all live under the
threat of foreclosure?)

After paying for the land and the lawyer's fees I would
have $12,292.90. I owed the yard $3,767.30 now. The
new money wouldn't go far. In any case there were papers to sign, insurance to take out; it wouldn't be all
completed till the end of the month.

Anticipating solvency, I wrote a check to the Yard, on
account, and ordered the aluminum roofing, twenty-one
pieces four by twenty-two feet. Also a whole mess of 2 ×
3's for studding the main floor. A 2 × 3 is not really a
sturdy piece of lumber, but that fall it was selling for
thirteen and a half cents a foot, and 2 × 4 for twenty-four
cents. The wall didn't have to hold anything up, but

served only to contain insulation, windows, a sort of curtain against the weather. We would nail the different sections of studding together on the floor of the barn, cut to fit in between the posts, rough openings for the windows included.

It was a good part of the attraction of the slim 2×3's that they were easier to saw. It was mostly by hand still, though the Juicers had sent someone over to poke a bit of steel in the ground. Of course they had found rock (I coulda told 'em). We would expect them back anytime, when someone found the right moment to do a job so insignificant. The man with the backhoe, the same gruff gentleman who had dug in the septic system, had made us a trench, sheering off two teeth on his shovel while losing an argument to elements of the same piece of rock. We could be hooked up in a trice.

No matter how much more efficient we might be with power, there was still part of me that was glad to find that they hadn't made it yet. The sky continued clear, and that was benefit enough, though the night frost had dulled the colors, red-ochre and yellows, a prompting to me where none was necessary. Up on the roof again, spiking in those 2×6's. We had to look for the rafters with the nails, not always easy, given their meandering character. The new, heavy lumber seemed to like the job however; I thought I could feel the roof tightening up with every hammer blow.

By now that roof was ground well trampled. I knew that, steep as the roof was, a sneaker placed down with care would not slip, that the high back wall was no more treacherous than the front. Indeed, since those days way back in the heat of summer, I had lost the fear of falling. Balancing up there on the roof ridge at the end of a noble, sparkling day I thought, if the dream has gotten this far, it may even be accomplished. It has been given to me. And if that is so, then for the duration I am immortal. The logic was impeccable and convincing, though I had no wish to put it to the test.

By Sunday we had the dormer sheathed, a partition for the downstairs room—but details now fade into a memory of the quiet forest floor, a weaving of translucent yellows and oriental reds laid out under beech and maple trees. Finally that afternoon the sky clouded over and a few drops of rain fell, like the cold touch of a dispirited lover. In the grasping darkness the barn was like a tree-house, and so quiet I could hear each leaf fall, so quiet it was almost possible to see the leaf detach itself and wonder why that decision had been made. It would have been fine to lie there, to let the body rest under a blanket of fallen leaves. Instead it was into the steel box and onto the conveyor belt.

I would be on the Atlantic coast the next weekend, no more work would be done till the 20th. Five more weekends beyond then before Thanksgiving; if I could take some time off, and if the Good Mother Isis continued her invaluable assistance, closing up, installing the stove, hooking up a drain to the septic tank—it all seemed possible. Let's see, if the electric was in when I got back, one day could be spent putting a pump down that well, and . . .

The farther I got from the site, the harder it was to remember what I was doing. Money—one thing I had not counted on was a payroll. Not that Skip was making anything: I had started paying him by the day, an unskilled laborer's wages given the long August afternoons. But that had been an easier life: the garden to shop in and no pressures. Now the days were shorter but tougher. Would it be better to try the rest by myself, at least after we got the roof on finally? (I couldn't see myself trying to single-handle that metal roofing, not if there was a breeze of any sort.)

Skip left before me; these weary logistical details were meant to keep my eyes on the road. But it was late, and I was not doing well. The road blurred. Where was I? A car right on my tail blasted its horn. I was over on the side of the road, that's where I was, white fence just off the starboard bow. I snatched at the wheel and pulled back the being that was preparing to depart my innards —at least why else that awful and immaculate hollowness inside? The car sped by, blinking its lights. It's King Caliper, and thank you. I guess I'd better not try to do without him, no matter the cost.

Autumn is different along the coast. The air is more brittle, sound carries immense distances. My wife and child and stepchild had rented a small pink cottage on a bluff, the sea in the distance and closed summer houses all around. The land is dry and sorrowful. The visit does not go well. We disappoint each other in unknowable ways, and I am found guilty, rightfully, of having transferred my allegiance irredeemably, as if some foreign power had risen out of the inland woods and seized me for its own.

I think: this salty, empty landscape has given me over; finally, these patient grey shuttered houses are no longer beguiling, strangers have subverted their integrity; they are all massage parlors now, and the rot is pervasive. Yesterday, just this morning from historical perspective, people lived here with the sea, glad of what it gave them, resigned to give back the necessary often bloodied sacrifice; now people who have grown rich because they were clever liars and unashamed persuaders come here to hear truth again in the pounding waves of a sea we have defiled, to gather shells that must be brought home and scoured before being put to the ear.

Nor was it the backdrop she would have chosen in a perfect world; there were compelling reasons to give it at least a try, perhaps to find an unoccupied but hospitable patch of humus in that sandy soil; friends, associations. Perhaps my reaction to her in her place is no more pertinent than her reaction to me in mine?

Except, except . . . Through a soft rain the boy and I visit the white church famous on its hill, from whence the parishioners once looked out at the cruel sustaining sea. It was a monument of my boyhood. (One night in adolescent midsummer, walking with the strange, warm girl/woman who inexplicably owned the key to my eternal happiness, crossing the fence there into the cemetery, moonlight on granite. Her hand in mine is Grace, Virtue. Dare I kiss her?)

Through the slim old headstones first. The indistinct lettering: "Died at sea," "Died at sea," "Whome the sea took for her own." This hand I hold is innocence, and my own, as we move slowly down a road between later, more ambitious monuments—rails around that one, a famous name's over there. The last time I was here the grave was not yet grown over; where is it exactly? Farther; remember that he wanted to look over the valley. There's the marker, that tree surprisingly small still, but yews don't exactly bolt. Or perhaps in this sandy soil the chemical value that was my father has already seeped down into salt water, leaving those hungry roots stretching in vain. It would be like him, my father. My gentle, thoughtful father, whose great life work was to destroy himself. Damn him, now that I miss him. How must I be to be a different father?

It has turned cold and misty, but it is necessary to free the tree of a twining cat briar. The boy, nineteen months old, is on my hip. We sit to do the gardening. He is unusually subdued in my lap, interested rather than surprised, I hope, by the pull of sadness, rising, rising with each half-held breath. Mist obscures the pines, there is no sky, only sadness reaching up from the grave, monumental.

Why must I keep this thing to myself as if I were on a deserted isle and it the last crumb of sustenance? I can not live on it forever. I am not inviolable, protected from the consequences of time ticking away, the lowering sun. I am in a hurry and I need help, and it is all right to need help (Father). On Friday I will leave the city early and pick up the stove. The four girls will join me, and I have asked that they bring any friend who can work. Also Lars, Skip, a woman I knew who needed this sort of therapy, I thought. That would make eight, perhaps more depending on the strength of the child-labor battalion. It would be a tight fit, but we would keep each other warm.

One thing this country can do is transport. Only a few miles from this reasonably remote antique store, there was the usual garage renting trailers: mine had Georgia plates. It wasn't much to back the thing right up to the porch, dismantle the stove and drive away. The fact that no one was there when I was doing it made me a bit nervous. It figured someone would show up; just please not a fired-up local policeman who might mistake my intentions. Then the minute I had managed to drag the body of the stove into the trailer (the only really heavy part) the owner showed. He took my check, and I rattled off down the road.

On the way there was a garage sale, where someone had it in for cast-iron pans, also a couple of pie plates, a big aluminum pot with a brass handle, and sundry knives, forks, spoons. A stop at a hardware store for six-inch metal pipe, two elbows. At the bus stop four girls and a bewildered man/child roped in by the eldest were properly impressed with the stove; it was venerable, no doubt about it. Likewise impressive was a studio bed tucked in the back of the station wagon.

We ate in town and laid our sleeping bags on the new concrete floor that night. The moving-in began in earnest Saturday morning. The stove was taken around to the back in the unhitched trailer. It was a job of a few minutes to put it in place in a corner of the windowless, doorless room. The pipe goes out through the wall, where we left off with the siding, just for now. But first, let's get the rest of the trim on. I ask someone to go out and get the last two pieces of trim for the front and one side. What do you mean? Of course it's there. Look, I know the stove was whole when I put it into the trailer. Perhaps it fell out while the trailer was bumping through the meadow. Nothing? Perhaps somebody looted the trailer overnight? No, not really likely. Could it be that I simply had not noticed that the most visible pieces of nickel trim, on the front and side of the stove, were missing? I guess I had wanted so much to see it complete. And, later, the store owner couldn't remember a thing.

I had worried about the pipe, not knowing how it worked. It comes in two-foot lengths, which you can put together as easily as a Tinker Toy. We only had trouble fitting the pipe around the old collar on the back of the stove. The collar is oval, the pipe is round; it's a simple question of geometry, but squeezing the pipe breaks its seam. A pliers then to cinch the metal more firmly; then a piece of wire coat hanger, that great all-purpose item, wrapped around. Now, is it that you need just stuff some paper and kindling in the firebox and put a match to it? It seems too simple to be right; fire is subtle, engrossing, such a complicated element. Are there no magic words to say, dampers to adjust? The paper burns as paper does, the slivers of spruce catch. When the lid goes back on, of course, the lazy fingers of smoke reach out of the stove, through all the cracks age has given it. It will never do. But from outside it seems as if there's a good deal of smoke finding its way out the pipe as well. Slowly, as the stove heats up, crackling with pleasure, the smoke stops rising from its surface. One of the kids tries touching it, naturally; yes, it's *hot.* How miraculous.

By this time the crew had arrived, come to work, not stand around watching an old black Standard start to cook. I left its low throaty rumble reluctantly. There was a certain briskness in the air, high clouds; the leaves were mostly gone, I see in the snapshots; the migrating birds, including once a large flock of geese seen in the distance but heard as if they were camping in the maples, had mostly left us. It was a quiet day, fortunately: those huge sheets of insulating foam weighed almost nothing, so that even the slightest breeze can rip one right out of your hands. The foam is also soft, can't be walked on directly, thus the sandwich (aluminum on polyurethane) went on in four-foot sections.

It was the aluminum that right away proved why it is that wood is such a valuable commodity ("It is remarkable what a value we put on wood even in this age and in this new country . . ."—Thoreau). We had gone to some trouble to find the longest possible nails, but they were 8-penny nails (2 1/2 inches long) not 10's as were really required. However the nails were spiraled for better holding power and came equipped with a blue plastic washer to seal the hole made through the roofing.

What's more, they were aluminum nails, easy to bend and hard to remove.

The giant sheet of polyurethane lay down for its long sleep, knowing its place. The 2×6's made it easy to climb up and down the roof, but how to tack down the far edge without putting a knee through it? Anticipating—the worry about the possibility of encountering the impossible, solutions without problems—I had knocked together a flimsy ladder with a hook at the top which could be laid over the ridge once the material was in place. How satisfactory that it was just the tool that was needed. How unsatisfactory that the sheet of aluminum had such sharp edges (careful you don't cut into the tender skin of the foam) and came with these brittle nails. It takes two sharp blows to punch through the metal with the nail, and then you better get that washer squarely seated.

I missed a few nails, bent them; this was an ornery sort of job, no question about it. These nails are not making it. Skip is even less impressed than I; we should substitute the 10-penny galvanized, fitting them out with the little blue washers from the first set. But we don't have enough of the 10-penny for the job. If someone hurries they can get to the store and back in an hour, or we could tack it down now and see if the Pragmatist might have a better solution for us. It is obviously too laughingly amateur to be doing it this way. So we'll get it all on and seek advice on nail manufacture. For all the wrong reasons that is exactly the right decision, as we shall see.

By the time we had gotten over to the south end of that front side, we had begun to know what we were doing, to appreciate the importance of handling the material carefully, lining it up, all the little things that are second nature to the person who has done it before. The beginning of any job is apt to be hectic if it's new, the unknown quotient gets in the way, demanding tariff; but then the someone who knew what he was doing undoubtedly wouldn't do this.

The sixth piece of roofing overhung the overhang, of course (4′ divided into 22′). I tacked it down, we got the car in position, turned it on, ran the long yellow extension cord with a sabre saw on the end of it up the ladder. We snapped a chalk line along the edge, and I got to work: a terrible noise, the aluminum bouncing and writhing, the saw almost requiring both hands to hold it down.

The blade is new, fine-toothed and listed for metal cutting. It tends to jam. After three or four minutes I have cut no more than six inches of the twenty-two feet. Plainly, this is not how it's done; but tin snips are not much quicker and less accurate. We should work on it on the ground, where whoever is trying to use the saw isn't hanging over the edge of the roof. Or should we try to rent a better tool from the place half an hour away that rents everything? Skip slyly points out that since the roofing is ridged we could overlap the extra. Cheating, I say, but there is a smile of conspiracy on the lips of the crew. It requires only that we end-for-end this piece.

On the backside we had to slip the pieces carefully around the eves, through the nonexistent walls. The kids had moved the camp uphill in the morning, now they lent us their hands and their quick energies, the man/child getting a chance to see that his six-feet-plus could be useful, provided it followed instructions. There was a good nip in the air as the sun sank, and we quit early. Without a word Lars began moving material around to close in the downstairs room, tack some plywood over the sliding door openings, cover what would be the bay window with three big second-hand storm windows I had picked up in a junk yard. A piece of plastic acted as a door. The table from the camp was covered with an old blanket, and the kerosene lamp sat on it, glowing away. By the time I had made a bench out of two maple logs and an old piece of 2×8, we were encapsuled, sheltered. Immediately the room began to warm up. The woman who needed therapy had arrived earlier, asked what she could do and gone for a walk. Now she came in through the plastic and sat down on the narrow bed, just as if she were walking into somebody's house. She looked through long black hair at our magnificent stove and said, "Does that boil water?" Later she left with the one and only flashlight.

It didn't boil water all that quickly, but the water (good well water in a big galvanized bucket) did boil if you got the pot well nestled down over the back of the glowing firebox. Have you ever cooked spaghetti with beet greens? The pasta turns a peculiar pink, but it tastes wonderful, and if you go for greens, mix these with tomato sauce. In the pie pan one of the younger girls essayed brownies, but they came out of the oven candy on one side and cake on the other. Later—after the stove got a serious cleanout—we would learn the secrets of wood-stove cooking. Or some of the secrets, because that stove liked to keep them to itself. Mostly it's magic; only if used with gross ineptitude can it produce a bad meal. Also it is self-cleaning, attractive, outlasts modern ranges, used only renewable energy sources. Nor need it be unbearable in the summer, if you trim your menu to the season, as our fathers did not. All this is well known, why the wood-burning stove went out into the garage so fast is a puzzling question. It is the one stove that supplies instant, surefire heat control: left side is high, right side is warm. To select the proper heat for your saucepot find the spot in between, and no need to look at the burner; watch the pot, where the action is. No need for a toaster either, or a griddle—cook the stove-cakes right on the lids; and the coffeepot stays hot without wires or further capital investment. What's this about low-heat cooking? The soup pot is always on the back of the stove; when you're hungry just shove it over a foot or so as you go by, sharpen the axe or sew on a button, and it's time to eat. Try a big roast in the oven all after-noon, with the fires really damped down and the oven draft half open. And potatoes in the ashes under the firebox. Or, or . . . It is magic, that's all, better than automatic because everything it does is done with a spe-cial good humor, an evident staunchness, balance.

That evening we hadn't enough plates, some ends of cedar were put to use, big enough to keep the juices mostly contained. (Later the plates kindled the fire; see what I mean?) But there was no improvising cups, so we used paper ones, the coffee is too good to care.

And later there is real hot water for the first time, heated in an enamel wash-basin; several people even washed the chocolate off their hands and faces. There was a general brushing of teeth, the cup of water passing from hand to hand, farther and farther into the woods. When the sleeping bags were rolled out, this strange, dark, kerosene-scented nest was lined edge to edge with people, hardworking people; pathetic, pretending not to hear the jet planes overhead, and holding tight instead —if at all like me—to an inalienable sense of promise.

VIII

The Revolution of Falling Expectations

Sunday morning, October 21st; waking early, worried about the weather. We have got to have just one more reasonably good day. A leaden overcast, with a slice of new-risen sunlight angling underneath. I hope it is still too early to bring in a verdict.

This gang will need a rich breakfast if I'm to get any work out of them, so off to the store for supplies, stopping at the well on the way—a splash of that water reinforces self-confidence, wakens the nerve ends. The soft, knowing coldness was still with me as I bought eggs, milk, bread and butter, and lastly the Sunday paper. What's this? Headlines suggested a coup d'état in the District of Columbia. The President had fired the good guys. Quick—the car radio. Nothing. Bombs would have to fall before those stations interrupted their regular programing.

The aluminum glows on the roof, the barn looks more like a bandstand than ever, but around in back it is a World War I bunker, stove pipe and all, lacking only the regimental flag over the plastic-sheeted doorway; or, better, the headquarters of a Yugoslav guerrilla force circa 1943.

No one has moved a muscle in my absence. I get the stove started, splitting wood loudly. The company groans and shifts about. What's happening, someone asks. It's too early. But I am so full of news I can't let them sleep, and call attention to the headlines.

Instantly the paper is devoured; indeed our emotional distance from the events of the Saturday Night Fiasco in Washington gave those events a more sinister effect than they had generally. If we'd taken a vote in the few minutes that followed I am sure this particular unit would have voted to march, or, had there been a village meeting to denounce the despotism of distant monarchs, we would surely have gone. Perhaps it is only because we were ourselves in a frenetic state of mind, but the paper was read aloud as breakfast got made (you can't fight on an empty stomach either), and Skip volunteered to sit in his car and report any further developments heard on the radio. Perhaps when a citizen's physical environment is fragile and changing, when there is real cause to doubt his ability to make it through the next winter, he is more sensitive to political events. Or, put another way, surrounded by the casual opulence we take for granted it is understandably hard to believe that politics makes any difference. Will the lights go out, the TV die? Central heating, hardware has become more important to us than government's drift toward a state of permanent technological chaos. Perhaps Jefferson was right the first time, and democracy doomed by the relentless machine in man, subsequent events notwithstanding.

For us, the staid comments finally heard on the radio were anticlimactic, though welcome. As a result, the work got started late and progressed only by fits and starts. It still did not seem as if this material had been a good choice, though perhaps when we got all the metal nailed down firmly and the ends cut with a proper tool, it would last awhile. In any case we got a cap on and the rest of the roof covered, but not the damned dormer. You see, as that metal is ridged, you can't bend it or tuck it up under the piece above, as you might a shingle. The dormer would have to be sealed with tar or something.

That is what I was trying to do the next afternoon. It had turned nasty. A northwest wind was blowing along the top of the pines, coming down from Lake Erie and the Canadian tundra, measuring the valley for snow. There were brief splatters of rain. Every once in a while the wind would hit the roof in such a way as to catch an edge of the metal and rattle it slightly. I had to give up on the job I was doing. It was the wrong time of day to try to be precise; we had laid some felt on the dormer anyway. I nailed down one piece of the metal temporarily after cutting it by hand. Skip was uncharacteristically scampering over the roof, getting more nails in it (still not the right ones). He had thrown caution into the rising wind, and I guessed he was more worried about the weather than I.

As the day ended, the wind seemed to subside. Still

that damn roof was going to be a problem; we ought to find someone who would give us authoritative advice about it. Skip thought it looked like something out of *Tobacco Road.* But it would keep the rain off, I said. "Wait till you have a hail storm," Skip said. "Break your mucking eardrums."

Alas, we didn't have to wait for a hail storm. Around eleven, after we had tucked ourselves into our sleeping bags, the piece of plywood we had in place of a door suddenly blew in. It was startling, to say the least. In the next gust we again heard the metal rattling at the northwest corner. Soon it was joined by another noise at the peak. "The damn cap's coming off," said Skip, without lifting his head.

Oh, damn. Damn damn damn. Pray, I thought. Ask them to leave us alone for a little while; we have done nothing to deserve a rending wind. Aeolus, Commander of All Winds, protect us from this errant zephyr; send us gentle gusts from the north, curling harmlessly over the hilltop. Or better yet, tell the four winds to rest up altogether; save up for winter. *Crack.* It seems as if that corner has broken loose somewhat. Will it have to be replaced?

We get up simultaneously, pulling on shoes. Get the rope, we'll tie the sonovabitch down! I'm up on the roof in a flash, the cold wet breath of destruction whipping about me. More nails! Get that rope over the loose corner, let myself down, down the slippery aluminum, hoping that Skip has tied the other end securely. (I remind myself that I am inviolable.) Damn roofing is ripped already. The nails are pulling out all along the edge, I see. Pass me a length of lumber, tack it down. My hand is bleeding. The wind begins to lift the sheet of aluminum on the dormer. *Crack.*

On the ground, both of us seem to be losing a bit of blood, the damn stuff is lethal. A general, all-around rattle in a new gust. Well. Maybe it will be all right. Anyway there isn't much more we can do *(rattle, rattle),* and nothing without taking a considerable risk: what would happen if one of those panels let loose while you were up there, catching you as it flew by?

We hadn't half settled in again before the first great boom rent the air. Exactly like sound-effects thunder, but louder and infinitely more damaging. It was to cry. And again, the huge rumble as the metal lifted up and subsided. But with each gust, the sound diminished as the aluminum was creased further. And then another great crack. The whole roof could be felt vibrating, and this time an echo sounded way down the field. Piece number one had flown away while piece number two was just getting started, as if the wind were determined to take the roof apart in seriatim. There goes the hope for a closed-in house this year, tumbling, doom-booming down the valley.

It went on for hours. With each hideous report, the house lifted slightly, then sank, trembling at every post. We were living inside a kettle drum, and Thor was drunk and spiteful. Would the roof itself blow off, planking and rafters and all while we lay down here helplessly, retreating farther and farther into the dark recesses of our sleeping bags? The worst noises were the rumbling echoes as a piece of metal bounced and bounded down the hill, coming to rest against some old, surprised apple tree. I saw animals being cut in two, the field ploughed up.

Sleep came as the wind died, and morning too, on schedule. I didn't want to look, but as the wreckage lay all about us that option was not available, as they say. God, there's one full piece, twenty-two feet long, wedged against a maple tree, three hundred yards away. And as far away as the village center people thought that there had been a strange sort of thunderstorm playing around the top of our hill. And the neighbor thought for a while that night that we were being strafed and bombed by some air force gone beserk. As indeed we were. It was, to put it plainly, awful. Awful!

Somewhat dazed, we went around cleaning up; there were only two pieces of roofing left on the roof. In some cases the nails had popped out (the washers still turn up in odd parts of the field, foreign and interesting); in others, the metal had just torn away, leaving the nails and their neat bits of blue plastic holding tightly to nothing. Miraculously the insulation was unmarked, or nearly so; a couple of gouges where ragged ends had touched down before cartwheeling off again into space.

By lunchtime the sun was out. As so often happens the furies of the night became less and less believable as the day progressed, and we began to look for a bright side. The roof was wrong anyway, we knew that. It's lucky that sheathing came off now and not in a mucking blizzard.

Skip had never liked it. Anyway the bank would probably loan you money to start again; after all they had an investment. The bank . . . ? Mortgage . . . ? There is something I'm trying to remember. *Insurance!* Am I covered? I didn't even know if the policy that the bank required had gone into effect. Quick, but with trepidation, to the store to call the agent.

They were helpful but unexcitable; yes, they thought I was covered all right. Were they sure the policy was in effect? Wait a minute. (Wait?) Well, yes, in fact the policy had been in effect a good seventy-two hours before the storm broke. The Adjuster was already on the road, but they would get word to him as soon as possible. In the meantime best not to fix it. I couldn't explain that there wasn't anything to fix, really.

I was dragging a piece of roofing through the field when the Adjuster arrived. This call was conveniently between two others he had to make. Had gotten the report off his radio only minutes after I'd called. Found it all right? Sure, he knew the place well, he had clients all along this road once. He remembered when the old place burned; New Year's Eve, he thought it was, and the volunteer fire department was kinda hard to round up. Yeah, and when the householder got back up the hill here with the fire truck, well, the house was pretty far gone.

I asked him if the insurance paid out. Oh, yeah. There were a lot of fires around here in those days, seems like, he added slyly. The Company was always paying out.

What about this mess? Truth to tell, the roof wasn't

nailed down as well as it might have been. We were kinda still working on it.

It seemed I could recover the complete cost of replacing the roof, less the fifty dollars deductible. But did we want to replace it or do something else? Did it matter, I asked, not enjoying the implication that the roof had not been 100 per cent sound. Well, he wouldn't put this stuff on a roof, he said; it's always blowing off somewhere.

I stayed over Monday to go back to the Yard. They had not really liked selling me the aluminum; people just don't put aluminum roofs on houses much. Well, it may have been a lousy idea, but it was cheaper. There was nothing for it now but start again, using asphalt shingles (wood ones were too damned expensive), which in turn meant laying down a half inch of plyscore as a base. We would have to nail through the insulation again, using spikes to keep the ply from slipping. Plyscore, new paper to cover it, the shingles and nails cost just under six hundred dollars. The other roofing had cost just over five hundred dollars. I was amazed. False economy, even figuring that it takes four times as long to put on the shingles. (At the Adjuster's suggestion I had included a salary for myself in computing the cost of the first roof, so in cash terms I was ahead of the game.)

It must be said that the Prince of Pragmatists went out of his way to avoid saying I-told-you-so. There was only a small tired movement as he leaned on the counter, a slight smile and shake of the head as he wrote up the order. Time is money; haste makes waste. In this business, it is the latter proposition that makes sense; and maybe time is not money at all; perhaps time, as some have thought, is imaginary. I tried to remember that in the weeks that followed.

As soon as Skip and I had the new underlayment up and papered—and that didn't take more than a day—I called around to find some help with the shingling. The local radio station had a buy-and-sell rides-here-and-there sort of on-the-air bulletin board. Would they broadcast a notice? But they thought I'd be swamped, and anyway they didn't do want ads. Off the air, the announcer said she'd call back in a few minutes and give me some numbers. She did, and two guys in their early twenties showed up as a result. Also a kid I picked up hitchhiking, who lived in the village, and a friend of his. It was a lot of payroll, but I remembered a summer month spent shingling a garage: the job was next to endless. It was time to go for broke.

We worked in teams, but Pavel, who had been teaching school until recently, turned pale at the top of the ladder, and almost had to be helped down. He was grounded. Brick, foulmouthed and fat and dead game, who had been doing one thing or another, including playing in a band, since graduating from high school five, six years before, worked with one of the kids, and Skip with the other, me alone along the edges, doing the cutting.

The morning goes slowly, but as it is reasonably warm we get a rhythm going, and a little competition. Taking turns going down the ladder for more shingles gives everyone a chance to kibitz on the others' work, and we can all land on Pavel, who is supposed to be cutting some stove wood but can't start the chainsaw.

It's a war of attrition, a matter of keeping at it, like picking blueberries, I say, as we crowd around the stove later. (The existential problem of my youth, when blueberry-picking was the low point of the summer: if no one blueberry makes any real difference in how many blueberries there are going to be in the pie, how come it matters if I put this berry in my mouth or in the pail? I was a hopelessly slow berry-picker until I resolved the problem for myself by an arbitrary rule: never eat blueberries out-of-doors.)

The kids had not brought anything to eat; nah, they weren't hungry. They edged toward the door; outside on the roof they do the work of a man, inside both of them, thin, looking undernourished, shy, seem ten years younger. But they have to eat something; company regulations: no eat, no pay. Reluctantly they take a little soup from the big pot, canned but with some of this morning's cereal swimming around in it. When you have no garbage pail, the soup pot is the beneficiary—another of Skip's Famous Sayings.

Pavel kept himself busy for those two days; with some urging he even tried carrying shingles up the ladder. It was not for him however, all the blood seemed to go to his feet. But what do you do if you're a teacher and there are no jobs teaching? Later I heard he got a job with a well-drilling crew. And the teenagers plainly enjoyed earning wages; there are few enough such opportunities in this part of these Great United States. They thought that once out of school, and if they could get themselves a grub stake, Alaska would be the place to make their fortunes. Massachusetts is still sending her sons West, it seems.

A cold snap came down that evening, and the next day, though clear as a ringing bell, was dominated by another fierce northerly wind. The shingles were heavy (approximately 2.8 lbs. per square foot, laid) some thirty inches long, with a gravel surface, "wood-blend"; but not heavy enough this day. The wind was constantly picking them up, wrapping them around our legs, splattering them over the hillside. To make matters worse, we had been sold one-inch roofing nails, too short for holding between thumb and index finger; it is necessary to place the nail on the shingle between index and middle finger palm up, tapping lightly to get it started. If your hammer is too aggressive on that first blow you soon have a couple of sore knuckles; if not aggressive enough, the nail falls before you can smack it again. It is particularly difficult in the cold, and gloves are incapacitating. Only early afternoon, but perhaps we'd had it for the day. I looked at Skip, to whom cold was a more formidable enemy; we could quit now, but was tomorrow going to be any better? There was still a depressingly long way to go to the peak. I thought of Yankee sailors making it around the Horn, charging up ratlines thick with ice.

And then, delightfully, an orange-juice bottle full of hot, sweet coffee appeared at the top of the ladder, and after it a friend who had appointed herself quartermaster. Nothing like it, not the coffee, but the unspoken urging-on. We did another course, and then another: the blueberry principle. And to rekindle the blood, down the ladder, shoulder a pack of shingles and up again, pretend you're charging San Juan hill.

I hadn't yet paid the Barnmover the last of his money. I almost did; he had said the last few things would be done before long, as soon as his next job would let him. We were missing a knee brace that was only a cosmetic necessity, inside sills, and four steel straps he said he would bolt onto the corners to aid rigidity. He may well have regretted that last promise, it was gratuitous and arguably not a part of the original agreement. Does one, this one, hold him to it? At the beginning of that summer I would surely have paid; now I paid a part, extending the carrot.

He came over pronto. Skip and I were fitting in the sliding doors when he strode through the main floor and put his head over the side. "What happened to your tin roof, Peter? Fly away on ya?"

"Yes, and why did you let me do it?" He, too, had thought the roof likely to give trouble, and admired the result of the trouble—the front was just finished. (Yes, for unforeseeable reasons the shingles sit easily on the Daliesque contours up above.)

The instructions that came with the sliding doors suggest that the installer might have something wrong with his ability to organize spatial relationships. I couldn't believe it was so simple. Actually, anybody who knows which end of a Phillips screwdriver does the work could do it. The people who make money putting these things together must spend a lot of time figuring out how to make them foolproof. Skip had done this sort of job before, he knew; but I wanted it to be difficult, to be challenging, and I was disappointed.

The trouble was, though I was sure I had one some place, we couldn't find a Phillips screwdriver. Skip said, Why not ask Bunyan up there? Ah, why don't *you?* It's your place—you ask. Quietly: because I hate borrowing tools. But I did anyway. He didn't have one either. Fine lot of builders. Finally his helper produced an old bent Phillips from the back of his (likewise) car. Beautiful!

Then it was just a matter of a few adjustments and behold, the doors are in, rolling back and forth on their nylon wheels just like California. The inside wall we sheathed with plywood for the time being. (I'm afraid some of it is still there, just in that one corner, you understand, where I haven't yet decided what the room needs.) A wood box, two long shelves supported by the bare studs; it was a serviceable room, and with insulation in the walls it might even be warm, I hoped.

There were not going to be any more luxurious accommodations here for a while, that I had to get myself used to. The schedule I had set before had no basis in reality anyway; I had had no idea, really none. But already the diminished ambition was returning dividends. I had planned this room differently: it was to have had two interior doors. If they'd been built, one would have blocked the eventual inside flue, the other would have eliminated a bathroom closet. I should have listened closer to the Preacher: "It would be worth the while to build still more deliberately than I did, considering, for instance, what foundation a door, a window, a cellar, a garret, have in the nature of man, and perchance never raising any superstructure until we found a better reason for it than our temporal necessities even." Windy, perhaps. But thereafter I never did make an improvement on this house without first laying it out, living with it a while, and remarking on how it worked.

For a couple of weeks Comrade Brick, who seemed to have nothing much else on his schedule, agreed to stay here with Skip to finish the studding, a job that was tedious but, since the window sizes had been figured out, required no further decisions on the part of the project's servant and master. During that week I got a phone call: "Hey, guess what? I'm calling from a white wall phone . . . *in the house.*" Finally! Just when I was getting ready to say no thank you to the electric company. It had required blasting to get the pole planted. Then there had been a lot of to-ing and fro-ing about the expensive, too shallow ditch: the Juicers wanted the cable put through a conduit to protect it from the underground workings of the earth. After some probing I had found that their specifications could be trifled with to my financial advantage. That being done, the cable had finally been hooked up to a temporary meter on a pole.

Power. Just two outdoor outlets, it's true, but it changed things, connected the house to the world-wide grid via computer. A kind of respectability I wish I could do without was conferred on the project. If a gravity-fed water supply had been available and a root cellar . . . But it's too difficult if you're not there all the time. Lamps need filling, chimneys need washing, the hardware is expensive now and gets stolen. Nevertheless it is a compromise on both sides. Electricity doesn't like me any more than I like it. The first time I plugged in my old saw, I got halfway through cutting a piece of plywood when the damned thing just up and stopped. Couldn't figure it out. Tried the light, it wouldn't work either. Called the Juicers: busy. (First time I'd used the phone too.) In the end, of course, we were told the power was out, the company apologizes, the break will be repaired as soon as . . . It *wasn't* the weather. I suspect a personal vendetta.

One product of the Great Wind and reduced ambitions was reduced options. Windows. The easiest way was the most expensive, but what the hell, it's only money: specifically $1,104.56 for ten welded glass casement units with removable screens. The detailing on these things isn't perfect, but they work; they're tight, and the trim can come off and be replaced (at least when the time makes itself available).

But I'm ahead of myself. We couldn't get to that part of the siding until the scaffolding came down. We discussed putting off the rest of the shingling, counting on the paper to last through the winter. I didn't like it, no one liked it really; it seemed right to get the shingling done while we were set up for it.

Ah, but the seasons don't wait on fools like me. It was winter cold. I picked up the two boys in their thin jackets early in the morning. There had been a heavy frost the night before. It lay on the ground like a great sheet; the west side of the roof wouldn't get any sun until midday, and it was frosted over. But up and at 'em, gang, no one lives forever.

What was I doing up there on the peak, looking over the clear still woods, the birches catching a bit of sun and shining back at me? Showing off, I suppose, esprit de corps, letting everyone know that if the old man could make it, it was really all right to do this strange thing at eight A.M. on a cold November morning. We had the rope tied to a post in front, and with that in hand it seemed safe to stalk along the the ridge and rappel myself down the frozen black paper to where Skip and the rest were arranging themselves for the assault. In fact, I could slide down to them.

The first time was fun. It seemed that here was a sport equal to skateboarding, without the loathsome equipment. Trying it the second time, however, was just stupid. The course was fast, the rope was wet. In a flash I was headed off the edge and into the woods some twenty-odd feet below. Try to land on your feet, dummy, I said to myself, stay loose. The King of Calipers was in front of me, studiously tacking on the metal drip edge. He heard my "Shit!" as I lost control, looked up, and, like a good middle linebacker, put his head down and caught me amidships, holding on to the edge of the roof. I bounced sideways, landing heavily on the scaffolding, facing in. This could be a spectacular circus trick, I thought.

THE REVOLUTION OF FALLING EXPECTATIONS

No one said anything for a while, but Skip knew, and I knew. It would have been a very nasty fall, perhaps for both of us. Later he said he couldn't remember what happened, just that suddenly I was banging down next to him. Perhaps the same person was looking out for both of us.

By the time we had used up those shingles, three work days later, we were beginning to be good at it, and it might be wished that we'd done the front side last. For one thing we used a slightly longer nail. When I'd gone in to buy another twenty-pound box the guy asked, "What length you guys been using?" There's a choice? "You've been banging your knuckles with the short ones, right?" Right. (I wonder who you have to know to be let in on their secrets?) For another, we rigged up a decent set of supports to hold material, tools, ourselves. The craftsman knows and always acts on the knowledge that there is no substitute for the right tool. It is always damaging in the end to try to get away with something—in this case chasing tools into the grass. (What happens then when the right tool doesn't exist? I suppose you make one. Perhaps it doesn't follow, but it is a practical truth nonetheless.)

One day the boys were so cold they were shivering in their boots, but they wouldn't wear heavier clothes, or didn't have them, nor would they borrow something of mine. Why is it a matter of pride to be cold, lean and hungry? I know that our famous Garbage Soup was inconsistent, and I rather wished that Skip would keep the eggshells out, strictly for aesthetic reasons, but it was damn nourishing and always interesting. (The cover for the pot was a piece of cedar, which gave the mix a unique, excellent and subtle *je ne sais quoi.*)

Thanks to the constant presence of the two Staghanovites, by the time we had tapped all our untapped resources to get the roof done, there was only the happy job of sticking on the outside walls and fitting in the windows. Happy because it's a job rife with instant gratification—as fast as you get one board up, the next comes on. And now that we had power! Well, it was smoke all the way. *Next!* Lay it up there and smack home that galvanized nail. Occasionally you have to half hang out of the wall, brace yourself, get a foot on an edge, applying sufficient pressure to take out the warps. *Next!* And someone would cut one wrong, and you think, .49 times 11'6", put it over there so we will remember to use it later, *Next!*

Another finding of craftsmanship: taking the trouble to do it right the first time or failing that, doing it right the second time. In contradiction, I am so frustrated by the initial failure, as when that length of cedar doesn't fit around the rafter end (most likely I did not pay close attention when I measured the cutout) that, instead of taking it back to the saw horse and re-sawing, I bang at it, trying to make it smaller by force, splitting the wood and making myself cross as an old boil. Lack of confidence surely; in a way, the kids are better at this than I. They know that haste makes waste, and time's dreadful passage does not shadow their days.

But the value of those days is greater than the lessons thereof. Closing in, *not* being able to see through, suddenly finding the wind blocked: shelter. And the wood particularly clean, easy to work with, always that bright smell. It has some knot holes, okay, trees have knots; it splits; it shrinks in the summer sun, so that I may sometime have to batten the exterior. But over all it is satisfying, it makes me feel clever, particularly as the price has, as of this writing, gone up to .70 a board foot.

All the children were there then; wife and boy too, driven from the bluff near the sea by the cold November winds. The stove heated and cooked, still with its pipe through the wall (as a result the large south-facing window had been left uninstalled so the draft wouldn't be interrupted), supplemented this weekend by an outdoor fire. The company was arranging itself within, sitting on benches around the table, reading, books held close, the kerosene lamp casting its soft glow discriminately, bypassing the makeshift walls, the cement floor, the rows of sleeping bags laid out on their thin mats. Outside, resting on pieces of granite displaced by this house, lamb steaks cooked over the coals of a maple fire, attended by my wife. I was conscious of her self-exclusion, unprepared for her entrance through that smooth-sliding door. She took my hand and led me out to stand in front of the south window. We looked together through the misfitting glass, as if through a scrim, at the set of a silent play. The actors danced across the stage slowly, laughter came from the back, rising like the steam from the magic stove, disappearing into the darkness of the beams overhead.

"See what you have done," she said, applauding.

"Yes." But it is not me, I thought, though she was right. It seemed a fine play indeed. Only our separate hungers plucked us away from it.

A few days later I sat down alone with my son at early evening, the last Thursday in November. The other actors had scattered. We had come in from watching the western sky turn from orange to crimson to a deep purple striped with gold, clouds like giant fish. He had wanted to walk to the stream, but the woods were dark and close, the field a safe retreat.

The big black stove wheezed and belched in its corner as if it knew the date and was disappointed to have nothing more in its belly than two large sweet potatoes. We stood for a while in front of it letting its heat draw the chill from our clothes, contemplating dinner. In the circumstances it seemed right to be sparing: eggs from a farm not far away, scrambled with cheese, and parsley picked by us both in the garden. Also our own carrots (not that their origins made any difference to my companion—it was all fuel to him). We sat at the camp table, he on the end of a beam, me in a chair Skip had put together to match the table—straight-backed, puritan. There was a candle and a bit of wine. We ate and ate, and when it seemed to be over the oven produced a kind of apple tart I had almost forgotten was there. I made a note to myself "Good food. Excellent company." Even more satisfactory than the dream are the modifications necessity makes, keeping alive the possibility of grace, heroism, being better than we are.

*　　　*　　　*

The mist rises on the new pond in the woods, where trout are to grow. It had dawned clear after a cold rain. A wet breath is blown against me by a breeze I can hardly feel, yet the wisps of cloud, like smoke, travel the mirrored length of the water at breakneck speed, then at the water's edge fall suddenly apart and vanish into the trees behind me.

In the soft earth by the stream there are the fresh tracks of a doe and her fawn. Yesterday a bulldozer was at work here, remaking what the beaver started so long ago. The deer must have been startled by the changing landscape. I can see where they stopped, turned, then came on again. The fawn is getting big now, its tracks no longer surprise by their smallness as they did in the spring. I'd like to catch sight of these two. Tomorrow, if the weather holds, I will come down here before light, find a spot on the other side of the pond overlooking the stream and the woods of their refuge.

It is so quiet that a truck changing gears on the hill to the town dump, three, four miles away, is a disturbance. There have been two kingfishers nesting close by this summer, and last week I came upon a heron motionless in the shallows, then watched it glide away through the dead trees at the head of the marsh. Now the only company is a noisy group of sparrows and a pair of hard-working nuthatches, scampering up and down the dead oak.

Something jumps in the middle of the pond, something big: perhaps that fish has taken to the pond to escape the attentions of marauding carnivores. In the quiet it makes two distinct sounds, each seemingly complete in itself, leaving the water and hitting it again. Studying the rings widening on that immaculate surface I am surprised by a rumble close at hand: it is my stomach telling me that it's time to break fast.

Back through the overgrown pasture, spruce and pine now thirty, forty years old, trees just taking root when I was born. The casual intruder might not recognize that this was cleared, working land so recently. But here is a gaunt, tottering fence post, part of a post-and-rail gate marking the way from open pasture into the primeval forest, almost impossible to imagine. The path that I follow was a logging road once, I think, though the ruts have been absorbed into the wet carpet of evergreen needles and club moss.

Here's the other fence line; if you look carefully you will see that someone planted a line of beech trees along it once. What hand, prompted by what motive, set them there? Living fence posts? An eye for history, the strength of the soil? And up the path, sitting a little awkwardly on the brow of the hill, there is a house. Is it too tall from this angle, do you think? heavy with glass and a dormer where no dormer should be? The cedar siding has weathered to a light brown, greyer around the doorstep where the rain drives into it. But some of the trim is almost new, giving away—if you hadn't noticed before—that this is certainly an amateur-built house.

The morning dew drips off the dangerous roof edge into the gutter. Inside there is a rumpled bed, tools on two different workbenches, walls covered with matched spruce and old painted siding from a collapsed barn down the road, other places where the silvered insulation still waits to be dressed. It's always a surprise when you turn a valve and water pours out of the faucet, hot too. (Perhaps the most effective argument for Modern Civilization is the commonplace of hot running water.)

No, that's not the magic stove: this one's much the same though in better repair and, as you'll notice, complete. The original was traded for a week's work. This one's prettier, but also more delicate: it is known to make mistakes, however, and I wonder about the wisdom of trading away that kind of loyalty for the sake of two pieces of nickel trim and the absence of a little smoke.

Yes, the windows in the gables were a splendid afterthought. Welded glass, they had to be made in a factory and cost too much. But it was making the frames that was the problem: every piece of wood had to be cut specially, all the angles were different. It took two of us two summer weeks and more; in fact, that's where the stove went. That first winter the gables stood open, snow drifting onto the plastic-covered floor. Christmas Day it was below zero at dawn. I had tried to close off those openings by myself, the day before. It had started to rain, then the rain mixed with snow, a bitter wind blowing up the valley. I thought: where there is a will there must be the resolution, and managed to tack a piece of wallboard on one side, remembering my awful fantasies of being exposed to unkind Winter. When I got to the southwest corner the storm was worse. I couldn't see, the wind hit the panel and knocked me kinda sideways. There was ice on the floor and the ladder slipped. Down we came; I was out cold for a while, not long though. I reckon it was the last chance the house had to get me. I've wised up since.

The chimney brick comes from a demolished mill in the Hudson Valley, and that slab of granite for the hearth from the old foundation. It was a doorstep once, I think, there are marks in it that look like chips taken out by horseshoes. It took three of us two days to drag it up here barely a hundred yards. Those slabs of pine on the kitchen counter are from the Home, and the trim around the doors is the 3×4 studs cleaned up with a plane. I forgot where that chair rail comes from; you do something like that and look at it for a while, squeezing every last drop of pleasure from it, and then one day it is simply there.

The door was designed by one of my daughters, or rather it was her idea; sunbursts are an old form. Careful on those stairs: they were temporary three years ago and as soon as I have a week they will be replaced. You're right, it had better be soon; another project that must wait for time, another change to anticipate, to look forward to. The house will never be finished, really. Or when it's "finished" there are barns to build, and a tower perhaps, just a folly for sitting in and thinking, dreaming new dreams.

I'm glad I didn't know then what I know now. This is not a job to contemplate in detail before the fact. Still if I had it to do again there are many things that would be different. The water underneath the bathroom floor is a standing monument to ignorance. And this floor isn't as solid as it should be. I don't know what we were thinking of back then; in love with the process I suppose, and you know what love does to good sense. The fireplace is not the one I wanted either; it will have to be remade. I could go on . . .

But none of its faults takes away from the joy of this place, perhaps just the contrary. Sometimes, especially in winter, I look with envy at other peoples trim, white houses, look through their curtained windows, wanting to share an existence that is unaware of wayward waters under the earth, and a spreading splice in the rafters. But I know that it wouldn't last, that this changing order, the constant searching for knowledge of some thing's mechanics, or a design that might for a moment seem clever, has an infinite value for me. How do you toenail two 8-pennies into the end of a stud to get the maximum use of the nails without splitting the wood? How is that mortise made?

Surely I am not unique in believing I can contain the bewildering complexities of our time by physical effort. I am completely knowledgeable about this house, as if I had x-ray vision. It is disquieting at times, but when the electricity goes off I know that I can still make do, that the wood stoves will give out heat, that I can lift water from the well as countless farmers have done before me —in a bucket. The preeminence of unmanageable, despotic technocracy, which breeds the paranoia of our times, is thus momentarily defeated.

I learned this at least, that pursuing an ideal can

not be put on a timetable, that the dog on the highway (radioactive perhaps? rotting and untouchable?) is a sure warning. We go so fast that we forget to honor the strength, the character of a valuable heritage almost destroyed in our flight toward the worship of sensuality. We must bring those attributes along with us in the same bag as the antibiotics and microcircuitry. We need to see, feel the difference between the chisel and the chainsaw; properly awed by the power and efficiency of the latter, we must not forget the simple elegance, the precision of the former—or that the chainsaw is a compromise, necessary not better, required by changes in our lives and our expectations of life. Neglecting this, we are doomed to a wasteland of Colonial Burgers, chocolate fife-and-drum rolls, plastic "hand-hewn" beams; the machine replaces spirit, empty pleasures replace the possibility of accomplishment. ("Our security has actually diminished as our demands have become more exacting; our comforts we purchase at the cost of a softer fiber, a feebler will, and an infantile suggestibility . . ." —Judge Learned Hand) We can no longer afford to arrange payment tomorrow, knowing that we die today. The planet has grown smaller, and our credit is running out.

And I have learned that tools are not magic, that they can work for me and you in the same manner as they work for someone who truly knows a craft. If wizardry plays any part—and I have a mind that it does—it is that in the use of tools, talent must have a sound knowledge of its limitations and the equivocal nature of inspiration.

You ask about the problem with the siding? Well, we

contrived a solution. It was neither easier nor harder than expected, and I believe it is sound. We will know someday, or at least the children will. I hope to live in comforting ignorance, advancing slowly in the direction of my dreams.

About the Author

PETER H. MATSON was born on Cape Cod, grew up in New York City, went to school in Connecticut and attended Harvard and Columbia. He started working in publishing while he was still in college. He is at present a literary agent in New York and a homesteader in Massachusetts.